VIOLENT ADOLESCENTS

Other titles in the
Forensic Psychotherapy Monograph Series

Violence: A Public Health Menace and a Public Health Approach
  Edited by Sandra L. Bloom

Life within Hidden Worlds: Psychotherapy in Prisons
  Edited by Jessica Williams Saunders

Forensic Psychotherapy and Psychopathology:
Winnicottian Perspectives
  Edited by Brett Kahr

Dangerous Patients: A Psychodynamic Approach to Risk Assessment
and Management
  Edited by Ronald Doctor

The Mind of the Paedophile: Psychoanalytic Perspectives
  Edited by Charles W. Socarides

Anxiety at 35,000 Feet: An Introduction to Clinical Aerospace Psychology
  Robert Bor

VIOLENT ADOLESCENTS

Understanding the Destructive Impulse

Edited by

Lynn Greenwood

Foreword by

Robin Anderson

Forensic Psychotherapy Monograph Series

Series Editor
Brett Kahr

Honorary Consultant
Estela Welldon

KARNAC

LONDON   NEW YORK

First published in 2005 by
H. Karnac (Books) Ltd.
6 Pembroke Buildings, London NW10 6RE

British Library Cataloguing in Publication Data

A C.I.P. for this book is available from the British Library

ISBN: 1-85575-915-2

10 9 8 7 6 5 4 3 2 1

Edited, designed, and produced by Communication Crafts

Printed in Great Britain

www.karnacbooks.com

In memory of Patrick Tomlin

CONTENTS

SERIES FOREWORD   ix

EDITOR AND CONTRIBUTORS   xiii

FOREWORD
  Robin Anderson   xvii

Introduction
  Lynn Greenwood   1

CHAPTER ONE
Understanding self-destructive behaviour in adolescence
  Andrea L. Scherzer   5

CHAPTER TWO
Beyond "bullies" and "victims":
a systemic approach to tackling school bullying
  Lucia Berdondini & Andreas P. D. Liefooghe   21

CHAPTER THREE
Parent battering and its roots in infantile trauma
    Reinmar du Bois   39

CHAPTER FOUR
Violence in care
    Bruce Irvine   57

CHAPTER FIVE
Working with adolescents who want to kill themselves
    Emily Cooney & Lynn Greenwood   73

REFERENCES   87

INDEX   95

SERIES FOREWORD

Brett Kahr

Centre for Child Mental Health, London
and
The Winnicott Clinic of Psychotherapy, London

Throughout most of human history, our ancestors have done rather poorly when dealing with acts of violence. To cite but one of many shocking examples, let us perhaps recall a case from 1801, of an English boy aged only 13, who was executed by hanging on the gallows at Tyburn. What was his crime? It seems that he had been condemned to die for having stolen a spoon (Westwick, 1940).

In most cases, our predecessors have either *ignored* murderousness and aggression, as in the case of Graeco–Roman infanticide, which occurred so regularly in the ancient world that it acquired an almost normative status (deMause, 1974; Kahr, 1994); or they have *punished* murderousness and destruction with retaliatory sadism, a form of unconscious identification with the aggressor. Any history of criminology will readily reveal the cruel punishments inflicted upon prisoners throughout the ages, ranging from beatings and stockades, to more severe forms of torture, culminating in eviscerations, beheadings, or lynchings.

Only during the last one hundred years have we begun to develop the capacity to respond more intelligently and more humanely to acts of dangerousness and destruction. Since the advent of psychoanalysis

x   SERIES FOREWORD

and psychoanalytic psychotherapy, we now have access to a much deeper understanding both of the aetiology of aggressive acts and of their treatment; and nowadays we need no longer ignore criminals or abuse them—instead, we can provide compassion and containment, as well as conduct research that can help to prevent future acts of violence.

The modern discipline of forensic psychotherapy, which can be defined, quite simply, as the use of psychoanalytically orientated "talking therapy" to treat violent, offender patients, stems directly from the work of Sigmund Freud. Almost one hundred years ago, at a meeting of the Vienna Psycho-Analytical Society, held on 6 February 1907, Sigmund Freud anticipated the clarion call of contemporary forensic psychotherapists when he bemoaned the often horrible treatment of mentally ill offenders, in a discussion on the psychology of vagrancy. According to Otto Rank, Freud's secretary at the time, the founder of psychoanalysis expressed his sorrow at the "nonsensical treatment of these people in prisons" (quoted in Nunberg & Federn, 1962, p. 108).

Many of the early psychoanalysts preoccupied themselves with forensic topics. Hanns Sachs, himself a trained lawyer, and Marie Bonaparte, the French princess who wrote about the cruelty of war, each spoke fiercely against capital punishment. Sachs, one of the first members of Freud's secret committee, regarded the death penalty for offenders as an example of group sadism (Moellenhoff, 1966). Bonaparte, who had studied various murderers throughout her career, had actually lobbied politicians in America to free the convicted killer Caryl Chessman, during his sentence on Death Row at the California State Prison in San Quentin, albeit unsuccessfully (Bertin, 1982).

Melanie Klein concluded her first book, the landmark text *Die Psychoanalyse des Kindes* [*The Psycho-Analysis of Children*], with resounding passion about the problem of violence in our culture. Mrs Klein noted that acts of criminality invariably stem from disturbances in childhood, and that if young people could receive access to psychoanalytic treatment at any early age, then much cruelty could be prevented in later years. Klein expressed the hope that: "If every child who shows disturbances that are at all severe were to be analysed in good time, a great number of these people who later end up in prisons or lunatic asylums, or who go completely to pieces, would be saved from such a fate and be able to develop a normal life" (1932, p. 374).

Shortly after the publication of Klein's transformative book, Atwell Westwick, a Judge of the Superior Court of Santa Barbara, California, published a little-known though highly inspiring article, "Criminology and Psychoanalysis" (1940), in the *Psychoanalytic Quarterly*. Westwick may well be the first judge to commit himself in print to the value of psychoanalysis in the study of criminality, arguing that punishment of the forensic patient remains, in fact, a sheer waste of time. With foresight, Judge Westwick queried, "Can we not, in our well nigh hopeless and overwhelming struggle with the problems of delinquency and crime, profit by medical experience with the problems of health and disease? Will we not, eventually, terminate the senseless policy of sitting idly by until misbehavior occurs, often with irreparable damage, then dumping the delinquent into the juvenile court or reformatory and dumping the criminal into prison?" (p. 281). Westwick noted that we should, instead, train judges, probation officers, social workers, as well as teachers and parents, in the precepts of psychoanalysis, in order to arrive at a more sensitive, non-punitive understanding of the nature of criminality. He opined: "When we shall have succeeded in committing society to such a program, when we see it launched definitely upon the venture, as in time it surely will be—then shall we have erected an appropriate memorial to Sigmund Freud" (p. 281).

In more recent years, the field of forensic psychotherapy has become increasingly well constellated. Building upon the pioneering contributions of such psychoanalysts and psychotherapists as Edward Glover, Grace Pailthorpe, Melitta Schmideberg, and more recently Murray Cox, Mervin Glasser, Ismond Rosen, Estela Welldon, and others too numerous to mention, forensic psychotherapy has now become an increasingly formalized discipline that can be dated to the inauguration of the International Association for Forensic Psychotherapy and to the first annual conference, held at St. Bartholomew's Hospital in London in 1991. The profession now boasts a more robust foundation, with training courses developing in the United Kingdom and beyond. Since the inauguration of the Diploma in Forensic Psychotherapy (and subsequently the Diploma in Forensic Psychotherapeutic Studies), under the auspices of the British Postgraduate Medical Federation of the University of London in association with the Portman Clinic, students can now seek further instruction in the psychodynamic treatment of patients who act out in a dangerous and illegal manner.

The volumes in this series of books will aim to provide both practical advice and theoretical stimulation for introductory students and for senior practitioners alike. In the Karnac Books Forensic Psychotherapy Monograph Series, we will endeavour to produce a regular stream of high-quality titles, written by leading members of the profession, who will share their expertise in a concise and practice-orientated fashion. We trust that such a collection of books will help to consolidate the knowledge and experience that we have already acquired and will also provide new directions for the upcoming decades of the new century. In this way, we shall hope to plant the seeds for a more rigorous, sturdy, and wide-reaching profession of forensic psychotherapy.

As the new millennium begins to unfold, we now have an opportunity for psychotherapeutically orientated forensic mental health professionals to work in close conjunction with child psychologists and with infant mental health specialists so that the problems of violence can be tackled both preventatively and retrospectively. With the growth of the field of forensic psychotherapy, we at last have reason to be hopeful that serious criminality can be forestalled and perhaps, one day, even eradicated.

References

Bertin, C. (1982). *La Dernière Bonaparte*. Paris: Librairie Académique Perrin.
deMause, L. (1974). The evolution of childhood. In: Lloyd deMause (Ed.), *The History of Childhood* (pp. 1–73). New York: Psychohistory Press.
Kahr, B. (1994). The historical foundations of ritual abuse: an excavation of ancient infanticide. In: Valerie Sinason (Ed.), *Treating Survivors of Satanist Abuse* (pp. 45–56). London: Routledge.
Klein, M. (1932). *The Psycho-Analysis of Children*, trans. Alix Strachey. London: Hogarth Press and The Institute of Psycho-Analysis. [First published as *Die Psychoanalyse des Kindes*. Vienna: Internationaler Psychoanalytischer Verlag.]
Moellenhoff, F. (1966). Hanns Sachs, 1881–1947: the creative unconscious. In: F. Alexander, S. Eisenstein, & M. Grotjahn (Eds.), *Psychoanalytic Pioneers* (pp. 180–199). New York: Basic Books.
Nunberg, H., & Federn, E. (Eds.) (1962). *Minutes of the Vienna Psychoanalytic Society. Volume I: 1906–1908*, trans. Margarethe Nunberg. New York: International Universities Press.
Westwick, A. (1940). Criminology and Psychoanalysis. *Psychoanalytic Quarterly*, 9: 269–282.

EDITOR AND CONTRIBUTORS

DR ROBIN ANDERSON, MRCP, FRCPsych, is a training analyst in adult, child, and adolescent analysis at the Institute of Psychoanalysis. He is also a consultant child and adolescent psychiatrist in the Adolescent Department of the Tavistock Clinic, where he was Chairman of the Department until 2000. He retired in 2003 and now concentrates on teaching and his private psychoanalytic practice. He has published papers and book chapters on adult and child and adolescent psychoanalysis and psychotherapy and has edited two books: *Clinical Lectures on Klein and Bion* and (with Anna Dartington) *Facing It Out: Clinical Perspectives on Adolescent Disturbance*. He has particular interest in early object relationships and the way in which they manifest themselves in later life, especially during adolescence, and he has applied this in working with suicidal young people. He has an interest in the way in which psychoanalytic work with children contributes to adult analytic technique.

DR LUCIA BERDONDINI, a developmental psychologist, is a Gestalt counsellor and Research Fellow at the Education Research Centre, University of Brighton. She has been working in the field of anti-bullying intervention in schools for many years, conducting research studies and practical intervention projects. She is involved in cooperative group work, communication skills, and group management for teachers at all levels. She also works with children in schools and specialist centres.

PROFESSOR REINMAR DU BOIS, MD, has trained in paediatrics, child and adolescent psychiatry, and analytic psychotherapy. He has been Principal Consultant in Child and Adolescent Psychiatry since 1985 and Senior Lecturer since 1988. In 1995, he was appointed Medical Director of the Hospital for Child and Adolescent Psychiatry and Psychotherapy, which was opened in Stuttgart in 1999. He has an extensive psychotherapeutic practice with severely disturbed adolescents inside and outside residential treatment settings. His main research focus is on the treatment of early schizophrenia within a supportive network both within and outside a hospital setting. He has written about early schizophrenia, developmental aspects of body experience in adolescent schizophrenia, adolescent crises, and anxiety in children. He is a founder and board member of the London-based International Association of Forensic Psychotherapy.

EMILY COONEY is a chartered clinical psychologist of the British Psychological Society, a licensed psychologist for the state of Washington, and a registered psychologist in New Zealand. She has interests in suicidal behaviour, eating disorders, and personality disorders and has worked with children, adolescents, and adults. She is currently working at the DBT Center of Seattle with adults and adolescents suffering from problems with emotion regulation.

LYNN GREENWOOD is a psychotherapist with a particular interest in adolescents and adults who exhibit behaviours that are destructive either to themselves or to others. She works at the Eating Disorders Unit at St George's Hospital in Tooting, London, at the Priory, Roehampton, and in private practice. She has also worked with adolescents and young adults at Huntercombe Maidenhead Hospital and with inmates of a major London prison. She teaches and writes on psychotherapy issues and has also acted as consultant psychotherapist for several television programmes.

BRUCE IRVINE is a Consultant Clinical Psychologist with more than 15 years of experience working with children, adolescents, and young adults in a range of settings, from high-security to community-based open-access services. He is Professional Services Coordinator for YoungMinds, leading a team of consultants and trainers working on projects throughout the United Kingdom. As professional lead and manager of a large Child and Adolescent Psychology, Psychotherapy and Counselling service, he contributed to the development of Child and Adolescent Mental Health Services while focusing on his clinical work with adolescents. He is an honorary lecturer at British and European universities, contributing to teaching of a wide range of professionals with regard to the psychological health of children and young people. He is a Senior Consultant at the Grubb Institute, UK, and a member of the International Forum for Social Innovation (IFSI), Paris, France. He works internationally within the framework of Institutional Transformation. As chair of the Voice for the Child in Care, he is particularly concerned with the provision of advocacy services to young people within and leaving the Care System.

ANDREAS P. D. LIEFOOGHE, BSc, MSc, PhD, C.Psychol (Occ), AFBPsS, an organizational psychologist, is a member of Faculty at the School of Management and Organizational Psychology at Birkbeck, University of London. He is a Visiting Professor at Chulalongkorn University in Bangkok, Thailand, and at the University of Iceland. He first worked with Lucia Berdondini on a five-year pan-European research project into bullying in schools. Subsequently, he developed and applied the school bullying work to organizations. As an organizational psychologist, he works with a wide range of businesses on issues such as bullying at work, executive coaching and organizational change programmes. His research interests include work on power and politics, morale in the armed forces, and the relationships between Human Resource practices and work and well-being.

ANDREA SCHERZER, BA, MSc, MA, worked as an education social worker before qualifying as a UKCP registered psychotherapist. She has a special interest in working with both adults and adolescents whose emotional problems manifest through self-destructive difficulties such as eating disorders and self-harming behaviour. She works as a psychotherapist at the St George's Hospital Eating Disorders Unit in Tooting, London, at the eating disorders unit of the Priory Hospital, Roehampton, and as a counsellor/psycho-therapist at an Inner London comprehensive secondary school. She also has a private psychotherapy practice in North London.

FOREWORD

Robin Anderson

Adolescent violence is an enormous problem in Western society at the present time. Nearly all violent crime is committed by adolescents (usually against other adolescents). This is often fuelled by drugs (a huge social and environmental problem in its own right) and is one of the forms of self-destructiveness from which adolescents suffer, together with suicidal behaviour and other forms of deliberate self-harm. Violence is one of the many symptoms of adolescent disturbance but is one that also evokes powerful feelings of fear and hostility in society as a whole, with a tendency, especially when the violence is against others, to provoke counter-hostility and calls for punitive responses.

Tackling this problem is one of the major challenges of our time, and, despite major efforts by many governments in the Western world, it remains endemic or is even increasing—and it is, of course, beyond the abilities of professionals alone to solve. However, what can be seen in *Violent Adolescents* is a very successful attempt to address the issue from two important standpoints.

First, the authors provide an impressive breadth of understanding of why adolescents can be violent. All of them stress that serious adolescent violence is borne out of earlier disturbance, often of a very specific nature, This includes an examination of the neurobiological features of aggression (Du Bois, chapter three) as well as of the circumstances of early developmental failures of containment. They also show how the particular stress of the psychobiological and social circumstances of adolescence lights up these dormant disturbances. Attention to the social aspects of adolescence includes an examination of the environment—the role of the *onlookers*, as Berdondini and Liefooghe (chapter two) put it, whether the onlookers are the rest of the class, the family, the housing estate, or society as a whole, caught in the familiar national clamour and excitement.

The other standpoint taken in this book is the question of what to do. Part of the fear and hostility that these young people provoke is, I think, a defence against the hopelessness and despair that we are required to experience. All of the authors have had to confront this in their work and in the preparation of this book, by finding ways of responding constructively and creatively to young people whose difficulties are often borne out of terrible circumstances. In other words, a starting point has to be the containment of projections of hopelessness and despair. The authors achieve this with great success, not to produce easy answers, but to show how it is possible to do modest and helpful work that can restore hope to these young people and help them back on to a better developmental pathway. In this way the reader will be refreshed and restored by the courage and care shown by the contributors to this book.

VIOLENT ADOLESCENTS

Introduction

Lynn Greenwood

Walking along the street between around 3.30 and 5 in the afternoon can feel daunting. As schools and colleges empty, groups of young people crowd the pavement, achieving what seems like an impossible range of simultaneous activities—eating, drinking, texting, and talking at top volume to each other. I always expect threading my way between them to present a significant challenge. Yet, even though they appear not to register my existence, they part to let me pass without missing a beat in their eating, drinking, texting, or conversation.

Adolescence is a time of change, discovery, and uncertainty. Erikson summarized it as a time when young people,

> beset with the physiological revolution of their genital matura-
> tion and the uncertainty of the adult roles ahead, seem much
> concerned with faddish attempts at establishing an adolescent
> subculture with what looks like a final rather than a transitory
> or, in fact, initial identity formation. They are sometimes mor-
> bidly, often curiously, preoccupied with what they appear to
> be in the eyes of others compared with what they appear to be
> in the eyes of others as compared with what they feel they are,

and with the question of how to connect the roles and skills cultivated earlier with the ideal prototypes of the day. [Erikson, 1968, p. 128]

Erikson was writing over 30 years ago. Adolescent rebellion has moved on since then. Or has it? In the 1960s, parents tut-tutted about their daughters' miniskirt or their sons' long hair. Then there was the music: no recognizable tune—nothing you could hum. The advent of the contraceptive pill meant that the risk of pregnancy need not inhibit sexual exploration, while marijuana and purple hearts heralded a new—"psychedelic"—culture. And, of course, there were the seaside skirmishes between mods and rockers.

In the early years of the twenty-first century, teenagers "negotiate" (or not) tattoos and piercings, and young women reveal an increasing amount of leg, midriff, and cleavage. Mothers complain about finding used condoms in their son's bedroom—or, on the other hand, worry that their offspring are not practising safe sex. The press devotes many column inches to the effects of ecstasy or crack cocaine—and the extreme violence of the lyrics of the latest gangsta rap hit (let alone the extreme violence of the performer).

Little has changed. Parents of adolescents brace themselves as the impact of hormones and a quest for greater independence kick in. Pierced belly-buttons, post-party drunkenness, and a heady cocktail of aggression, depression, and contempt are par for the course. In effect, young people renegotiate a transition similar to that of toddlerhood, when physiological and emotional changes create what can seem like an all-encompassing confusion.

Ladame and Perret-Catipovic (1998) argue that "[t]here is no adolescence without a crisis of adolescence" (their italics):

> In outline, the crisis accompanying the period of pubertal transformations culminates, in favourable cases, in a higher level of organization and psychic functioning than before. This gain is reflected, in particular, in greater autonomy with respect to the outside world and better self–other differentiation. The unfavourable outcome, betokening the onset of pathology and its retinue of associated symptoms, is a regression to modes of functioning inferior to the pre-crisis forms. Between these two extremes may lie an intermediate position that is by definition unstable: a kind of endless crisis state in which both

> progression and regression beckon but each of these paths is
> blocked by an insurmountable barrier. [p. 162]

Generally, adolescence is a somewhat ill-defined period that starts around the age of 12 and ends in the mid-twenties. Occasionally, events can take an altogether darker turn. No one would argue that drug or alcohol dependency are part of "normal" development. And sometimes adolescent anger and moroseness turn into repeated acts of delinquency or—sometimes fatal—violence towards self and/or others. I have worked with some disturbed patients in their thirties and forties and even older who have failed to negotiate this period and are "stuck" in a limbo between childhood and adulthood.

Working in specialist adolescent settings, I am all too aware of the "insurmountable barrier" created by what Ladame and Perret-Catipovic call the "endless crisis state". Sometimes a relatively brief stay is enough for a young person to "give up" her eating disorder—a destructive behaviour that impedes her progress into adulthood and the wider world. At other times, patients ping-pong in and out of hospital, often expressing a desire for recovery that they find impossible to maintain. Then there are young people living under lock and key in an intensive care unit and receiving the level of attention granted usually only to babies and infants.

James Gilligan (1996) has underlined the role of shame as a catalyst for violence. Adolescence is a time when feelings of shame can be at their height as physical and emotional changes often seem to threaten any sense of equilibrium. Blos (1962) views adolescent violence as a way of avoiding a sense of helplessness and of "counteract[ing] the regressive pull to passivity". In short, it becomes a defence against a sense of isolation, rejection, depression, and shame.

A crowd of noisy, boisterous adolescents can be intimidating. Being threatened by an angry young person (perhaps with fists or a weapon) is frightening—as is seeing the wounds that an individual can inflict on herself (or himself). Time was when it was generally assumed that males turn violence outwards and females inwards. I believe that this is changing. I have worked with young men who self-harm or have eating disorders and young women who have caused significant harm to others. Whether towards self or others, adolescent violence is an indication of extreme distress, often with origins within the family and perhaps exacerbated by school, work, and broader social situations. To support our young people as they make their way into an often confusing and difficult world, we need to tackle their distress in each of these environments.

CHAPTER ONE

Understanding self-destructive behaviour in adolescence

Andrea L. Scherzer

The term *self-destructive behaviour* is at once nebulous and provocative. For example, being late for work or school and raising blood-pressure and stress levels could be seen as self-destructive, as could the more obvious problem of developing a drug habit. The term also conjures images of adolescent rebellion, and often it does begin in adolescence. For adults and teenagers, behaviours that have potentially negative implications for both mental and physical health also serve a defensive, protective purpose and therefore hold a compelling attraction from which it can be difficult to detach themselves. This chapter links emotional deprivation—which can include neglect as well as over-identification by the parent with the child—in childhood with a tendency in adolescence towards employing self-destructive strategies to cope with difficult emotional experiences.

Adolescence is a confusing time of experimentation and testing boundaries, so it is not unusual for teenagers to engage in activities that might be seen by the adults around them as risky. Giving acted rather than spoken messages—often about anger and disappointment—is also a common feature of adolescence. However, there is a significant distinction between teenage acting-out and deliber-

5

ately physically hurting oneself in order to avoid confronting psychic pain. The term *self-destructive behaviour* has many possible interpretations, but in this chapter it is used to refer specifically to eating disorders and to the practice of deliberately wounding the body through activities such as cutting and burning, which is generally defined as *self-harm*.

Eating disorders and self-harm have been chosen because they seem to be increasingly prevalent in the adolescent populations of Western cultures and often occur simultaneously. In addition, these particular physical manifestations of emotional distress can be the first indication that a parent, carer, or educational professional has that a young person is suffering. Although such behaviour raises serious concerns for the adults involved, it is important to note that not all self-destructive adolescents have deep-rooted psychopathological disturbances and that for some emotionally deprived teenagers a self-destructive activity might, in fact, offer an otherwise non-existent experience of feeling purposefully alive. Furthermore, in my experience, many of these troubled young people respond positively to therapeutic support and to a sense that their feelings have been understood, respected, and contained.

The material described in this chapter is informed by my experiences working as a psychotherapist at a National Health Service (NHS) inpatient eating disorders unit, a private outpatient eating disorders unit, and at a comprehensive mixed secondary school, all in the Greater London area. Because much of this work takes place within multidisciplinary settings, my knowledge and expertise have been greatly informed by the contributions of dedicated and talented colleagues. My theoretical perspective comprises a combination of psychoanalytic, existential, and cognitive theory and practice.

Defining self-destructive behaviour

Eating disorders and self-harming behaviour have histories that significantly pre-date the twentieth and twenty-first centuries. Anorexia can be traced back at least to the Middle Ages, when prolonged fasting in women was linked either to religious piety or to satanic possession (Brumberg, 1988).

Bulimic behaviour was noted during Roman times, and the earliest case of self-harm is thought to have been described in Herodotus, Book 6 (Favazza, 1987). However, although these self-destructive behaviours are not new, the general public has become more aware of their existence in the last decade due to an increase in media attention and to the rapid expansion of communication technology. Thus it remains unclear whether more young people than ever are deliberately damaging their bodies in an effort to negotiate difficult feelings or whether this phenomenon is simply being more readily reported.

Similarly, much of the research undertaken concerning these behaviours in adolescents pertains specifically to the female population. Again, it is difficult to clarify whether more teenage girls are involved in self-damaging behaviour or whether they are simply more likely to admit to and talk about their distress than are their male peers. Psychoanalysts and sociologists have long pondered gender differences in emotional expression, and some have suggested that boys are more likely than girls to express their aggression externally due to differences in genitalia and physiology and/or that differences in emotional expression exist as a result of societal expectations that are gender-specific (Blos, 1962; Erikson, 1950; Gilligan, 1982). It is my experience that teenage girls feel more pressure than boys to adhere to physical ideals (which are often exacerbated through the media) and may attack their bodies as a result of feeling unable to achieve omnipotent perfection. At any rate, the statistical information that follows pertains mainly to female adolescents, but, rather than this being a sign that boys do not suffer from these conditions, it highlights a discrepancy in the information that is available concerning gender differences and self-destructive behaviour.

Despite a lack of clarity and agreement over the cause and treatment of eating disorders, it is generally agreed among practitioners that they are more prevalent in the female population, that they often begin in adolescence, that they involve disturbances in eating habits and in relationships to food, that they are often accompanied by distortions of body image and low self-esteem, and that they arise and persist for a number of complex reasons, the most prominent being disturbances in emotional development (Brumberg, 1988; Farrell, 1995; Levens, 1995). Recent statistics indicate that one in five women will develop an eating disorder, and that up to 80% of women are preoccupied with, or are overly concerned about, weight and dieting and are considered to be suffering from what is termed sub-clinical eating disorder (SED) (Farrell, 1995, p. xi).

Anorexics will often have intentionally lost at least 15% of their normal body weight, will have ceased menstruation as a result, and will have developed an irrational, morbid fear of becoming fat (Levens, 1995, p. vii). Bulimics engage in a cycle of bingeing and self-induced vomiting, abuse of laxatives and/or diuretics, and excessive use of exercise in order to control weight. Furthermore, based on their research, in 1986 Lacey and Evans proposed another subheading under the category of eating disorders, to include the "multi-impulsivist". This term refers to women who, along with a restricting and/or bingeing/purging eating disorder, might also abuse alcohol, use narcotics, shoplift, and mutilate themselves.

It is generally agreed that, as with eating disorders, self-harm often begins in adolescence, is repetitive and chronic, and can be accompanied by a temporary experience of depersonalization (Favazza, 1987; van der Kolk, Perry, & Herman, 1991). Although attempts at self-harm sometimes result in death, in most cases suicide is not the intended outcome (Pattison & Kahan, 1983; Tantam & Whittaker, 1992). A concise definition of self-harm has yet to be agreed upon, and therefore a proliferation of terms used to describe this behaviour includes wrist-cutting, self-poisoning, parasuicide, self-mutilation, self-injury, self-wounding, deliberate self-harm, self-laceration, and self-abuse (Warren, 1997, p. 5).

Interestingly, self-harm is frequently found in the predominantly female eating-disordered population, with studies reporting 35% of anorexics and 40.5% of bulimics admitting to some sort of self-harming behaviour (Cross, 1993; Favazza, 1989; Jacobs & Isaacs, 1986). Statistics show that in adolescents and adults aged 15 to 35 there are approximately 1,800 self-harmers per 100,000 of the general population, although the professional consensus is that incidences of self-harm are grossly under-reported (Favazza & Conterio, 1988; Warren, 1997).

Much of the research into self-harming behaviour suggests that it is largely a female practice, although young men are more likely to commit suicide (Warren, 1997). The most common reason women give for self-harming is to relieve unbearable emotional tension, anxiety, and anger (Arnold, 1995; Favazza, 1987; Gardner & Gardner, 1975). As with eating disorders, research shows a strong connection between experiences of abuse or neglect in childhood and the development of self-harming behaviour. Favazza (1987), van der Kolk, Perry, and Herman (1991), Miller (1994), and others have suggested that sexual abuse in childhood is a key determining factor in the development of self-harming behaviour. In her 1995 study, Arnold found that 49% of respondents reported sexual abuse in childhood, with a further 49% reporting the same for emotional neglect, and 43% reporting emotional abuse as a triggering factor. In their 1988 study Favazza and Conterio reported that 54% of female self-harmers used the adjective "miserable" to describe their childhoods, and in their study of self-destructive behaviour, van der Kolk, Perry, and Herman (1991) found that major disruptions in parental care were reported by 89% of self-harmers.

Self-destructive behaviour
and "normal" adolescent development

In order to avoid unnecessarily labelling all self-destructive behaviour as pathological, it is important to understand it within the wider context of adolescent development, as this period of time brings with it many complications, however mentally healthy an individual might be. One of the key aspects of adolescent development is identity formation. In infancy and early childhood we largely understand ourselves as extensions of our parents. Once we are of school age and undergo the increasingly complex process of socialization, our sense of our own individuality becomes influenced by relationships outside as well as inside the family. However, it is not until the physiological changes of puberty kick in that we are forced to grapple with—or attempt to avoid—the notion of ourselves as separate, sexual entities. At this point it can feel as though the bodies we have known and inhabited for 10 or 12 years have begun to betray us and that our emotions are now under the control of some alien force.

The hormonal shifts that accompany puberty necessitate a re-negotiation of ourselves in relation to others, which is further complicated by an internal conflict between craving the autonomy of adulthood and fearing the loss of childhood. The paediatrician and psychoanalyst W. D. Winnicott aptly described this chaotic time by stating that "adolescence itself can be a stormy time. Defiance mixed with dependence, even at times extreme dependence makes the picture of adolescence seem mad and muddled" (1965, p. 242).

The issue of sexual development is complex but requires some discussion here, as it has clear links to puberty, aggression, and therefore to violence and destructive behaviour. Freud originated the link between psychic experiences of infantile sexuality and adult sexual identity. His instinct theory of human psychological development was based largely on biology, although through his concept of the Oedipus complex he acknowledged to some extent that however instinctive human sexual development might be, it necessarily occurs within the context of relationships (1924d).

Basically, the Oedipus complex suggests that an intimate psy-chosexual bond develops between mother and infant son (it was Freud's contention that girls experienced a slightly different ver-sion of the Oedipus complex). Because she is physically as well as emotionally close to her baby, the mother becomes the recipient of his unconscious infantile sexual feelings and fantasies. As the child grows older and becomes aware of his genitals as a source of sexual pleasure, he initially assumes that mother will address these needs as well. As he grows increasingly aware that this desire is disap-proved of by his parents, this leads to the development of feelings of shame, guilt, and self-consciousness. He also begins to realize that it is his father, not he himself, who is the recipient of his mother's sexual attention. This raises complex internal conflicts about love, hate, and rage, which can be difficult to negotiate. If the support and love of his parents is sufficient, then the boy will eventually resolve this conflict by developing psychic strategies that help him to defend against the confusion and to put in place a psychological code of morality (superego), which he absorbs from his parents and from societal expectations (Likierman & Urban, 1999).

For girls, the process of working through the Oedipus complex is different, as she and mother share the same gender. According to Freud, the female child must relinquish her desire for a penis, tolerate her rivalry with mother for the affection of father, and ultimately take father on as her primary object in order to accept her feminine sexuality. As with boys, girls also have to negotiate complicated feelings of love, hate, envy, and rage and thus also develop defensive and moral psychic strategies in order that "forbidden" desires remain unconscious (Freud, 1924d). Managing rivalrous feelings with mother is all the more complicated in adolescence as the girl is likely to have to contend with mother's envy towards her youth and burgeoning sexuality.

The aggressive and guilty feelings that arise as a result of the Oedipus complex often lead to anxiety and conflict that can be experienced as unbearable and therefore need to be defended against. Fundamentally, having to tolerate simultaneous feelings of love and hate within intimate relationships is a core human dilemma and one that becomes intensified from puberty onwards.

Thus, in adolescence the task of managing rageful feelings becomes increasingly two-fold. On a physiological level sexual and aggressive urges increase, and on an emotional level unresolved issues from childhood can serve to impede an individual's ability to avoid being overwhelmed by his or her aggression. Violent and destructive behaviour are fairly obvious symptoms of unresolved rage, and for some young people turning that rage against themselves can become a coping mechanism in the face of inadequate or non-existent support in the family. It should be noted here that aggression is (within reason) a fairly healthy aspect of human emotional experience. It is also important to point out that although rage and self-destructive behaviour have murderous, deadly connotations, they can also be understood as aspects of human expression that are very much *alive*. Thus, rather than this behaviour being indicative of a desire to eliminate oneself, in many cases it is a reminder to the individual and to others that they are very much alive, with intolerable emotions.

Developmental disturbances

The psychic and physiological processes of puberty and adolescence can be confusing and complex even for the best-adjusted young person. Add to this equation not only the unresolved issues an individual might have carried from childhood into adolescence, but also any unresolved psychic dilemmas his or her parents might have, together with the various problems posed by the complexity of family dynamics, and it becomes more understandable why self-destructive behaviour in adolescence is not uncommon.

Because the role of parent is so essential in terms of helping to form a child's character and sense of self, when things go wrong the psychological damage is often complex and difficult to undo.

At the risk of sounding mother-blaming, it is important to consider the potential effects on a child's psychological and emotional development when his or her relationship with a primary object—more often than not the mother—is experienced as rejecting. I want to briefly examine this process from the perspective of object relations theorists such as W. D. Winnicott, and W. R. D. Fairbairn, because their belief that human motivation emerges from an innate need to relate and attach to objects (primary carers) helps to explain why some individuals take their aggressive feelings out on themselves when primitive attachments have been problematic or not possible. Winnicott noted that, philosophically at least, an infant's ego exists only in a potential sense, since it is activated and brought into being only in the context—and through the agency—of maternal handling (Likierman & Urban, 1999, p. 27).

In particular, Fairbairn described a natural sequence of stages of needs for various kinds of relatedness with others. He believed that if a mother is able to distinguish her own needs from her child's and is still able to instil in him or her a sense of being loved and cherished, then there is a good chance that the child will successfully move though each stage and develop into an emotionally healthy adult. The catch here is that Fairbairn believed that such unconditional maternal love is only idealistically possible, given the emotional stresses and strains of daily life. In this context, he and Winnicott believed that human mental heath exists on a continuum. By this they meant that most of us are prone to some sort of distorted thinking and/or respond to difficult situations in less than healthy ways, but it is the severity of the early trauma, together with an individual's personality, that dictates the person's ability to cope with psychological as well as environmental problems (Fairbairn, 1952, pp. 34–35).

One of the psychological outcomes of emotional and/or physical deprivation and abuse is *narcissistic disturbance*. Because of our innate belief as infants that we are the centre of our mother's universe, when we begin to recognize on a psychic level that this is not true, we suffer narcissistic wounding. As children, we all struggle to accept that we are not the only important object in our primary object's life. After all, it is a natural human desire to want to feel special to a significant other. When good-enough parenting has occurred, these wounds heal for the most part, and we are able to healthily manage the rage we feel as a result of having to lose an infantile sense of omnipotent control over the feelings of others.

When good-enough parenting has not been experienced either through neglect or over-identification, an individual must resort to developing psychic defences against this loss. Without the emotional support of a primary object to enable us to maintain positive self-esteem and trust despite disappointment, we expend tremendous psychic energy in an attempt to avoid having to feel rejected and disappointed. Whenever these feelings emerge in future relationships or experiences, the trauma of the original rejection is reignited. Thus, narcissistically wounded individuals struggle to accept the separateness of others and will often experience their own separateness as intolerable. As a result, such individuals may become very isolated in order to avoid this conflict or may become so pathologically attached to others that the ability to sustain healthy relationships becomes impossible.

The anger that narcissistically disturbed individuals experience for feeling rejected has to be repressed in some way. This means that these individuals are left carrying a dangerous amount of unresolved murderous rage, which feels unacceptable because it is secret and because it has not been contained by the primary object. Fairbairn suggested that one way of managing these difficult feelings is to maintain internal relations with "bad" aspects of our primary objects in an effort to attempt omnipotent control over an unbearable situation. This gives us the illusion that gratifying relations with a real or idealized parent can be achieved, as all the "badness" is hidden within oneself (Fairbairn, 1952).

Clearly, this is a self-destructive process. Where irreparable narcissistic wounding has necessitated the internalization of the "badness" of others, the individual is left having to manage the accompanying angry feelings. Not surprisingly, as an emotionally deprived child moves into adolescence and as his or her thinking becomes more sophisticated, he or she will need to employ increasingly complex and often destructive methods of coping with and defending against these feelings. I believe that developing an eating disorder and/or self-harming could be seen as examples of acting out anger both towards oneself for not having made things better and towards the primary object for not having loved well enough.

Furthermore, in a 1969 paper Kafka applied Winnicott's concept of a *transitional object* to self-harmers. Here Winnicott suggested that toddlers gradually transfer some attachment feelings from the primary care-giver to a tangible object such as a special blanket or toy. He felt that where the original relationship has been good-enough, the need for a transitional object eventually recedes, because the psychic representation of unconditional love can withstand separation (Winnicott, 1953). Kafka's theory, with which I agree and which can, I believe, also be applied to adolescents with eating disorders, claims that, at least for some self-destructive young people, the act of abusing their own bodies, often in a ritualistic fashion, serves a purpose not unlike that of a more conventional transitional object. For example, the process of inflicting pain upon oneself often has a brief anaesthetizing effect, which temporarily provides comfort from psychic pain. Kafka linked this need for comfort and reassurance in self-harmers to traumatic or precarious experiences with early attachments.

In summary, from infancy on we all need to feel psychically and emotionally connected to a primary object in order to develop into secure, autonomous individuals. For those whose earliest relationships were rejecting, suffocating, or traumatically severed, the need to give oneself a [false] sense of connectedness does not dissipate. However because the fantasy of the desired relationship does not match the painful reality of the actual relationship, destructive psychic defences must be created in order for the individual to pretend that all is well. Self-destructive behaviour can be utilized in an effort to act out rage towards the self as well as towards the object who disappointed, and to re-create a physical and emotional experience of pain and rejection, which provides a distorted sense of connection to a (negative) psychic representation of the primary object.

Linking self-destructive behaviour and emotional deprivation

A certain amount of emotional distress and rebellion is to be expected on the part of every adolescent, and as long as he or she is helped to manage these problems pro-actively, things should be fine. This is particularly true in terms of dealing with loss, which for many of us first occurs in adolescence in terms of losing childhood, losing innocence, and losing a sense of control over our relationships. Where good-enough parenting has occurred, the young person can be helped to accept and manage this loss in a positive manner. Obviously where emotional deprivation has occurred and/or in situations where the primary care-giver is unable to separate from the young person, the issue of loss cannot be addressed and must therefore be avoided and defended against at all costs.

Not surprisingly, fear of loss and separation are key factors noted in narcissistic disturbance and self-destructive behaviour. A sense of neglect and abandonment has been established as a strong precipitant in self-harming behaviour and is indicative of a fear of separation. Van der Kolk, Perry, and Herman found a strong correlation between experiences of separation from parents, environmental chaos, and physical and emotional neglect and self-destructive behaviour (1991, p. 1667). Pao also found that although several conflicts seemed to contribute to the initiation of cutting, problems over separation were most significant (1969, p. 202).

Walsh and Rosen emphasize narcissistic disturbances in the emotional development of self-harmers, which often occur as a result of experiences of loss or abandonment and severely distort their capacity for object love. Thus, actual or perceived loss in adolescence or adulthood reactivates the pain of the childhood loss and leads to self-harming behaviour:

> The role of loss, therefore, is that it triggers a regressive sequence in which, at the outset, the failure to achieve object love is re-experienced. The new loss is so troubling because a secure form of object love has never been attained. This makes the experience of subsequent separation and loss intolerable . . . and results in the profound, mounting, intolerable tension that cannot be verbalised. [Walsh & Rosen, 1988, p. 185]

Fear of loss and separation have also been found to be prominent underlying issues in the aetiology of eating disorders. For example, from the late 1960s and 1970s on the focus of causation in eating disorders shifted from oedipal to pre-oedipal disturbances, and failures in the phase of separation–individuation came to be seen as pre-eminent in the development of both anorexia and bulimia. Bruch was instrumental in recognizing this shift and noted that "even more confusing to the [eating-disordered] child are the actions of a mother who is continuously preoccupied with herself; whatever a child does, it is interpreted as expressing something about the mother" (Bruch, 1973, p. 56).

Stern has suggested that in many sufferers of eating disorders the denial of, and defence against, primary needs that have not been met becomes a developmental fixation because of the "parent's difficulty in responding affirmatively to the child's normal separation–individuation process" (1991, p. 101) Humphrey has looked at the object relations of family dynamics in eating-disordered patients and believes that the emerging individuality that occurs in adolescence is experienced as threatening by some families with an eating-disordered member. Similarly, in keeping with her emphasis on the influence of the mother's narcissism in the development of eating disorders, Farrell notes that although the child's lack of ability to separate from mother is essential, it is the mother's pathology that is the key issue (Humphrey, 1991, p. 43).

Fundamentally, when denial, defence, and pretence pervade an individual's inner world, the need for secrecy becomes paramount. Secrets and lies are to some extent a normal part of adolescent experimentation with autonomy and rebellion. However, lying about what one gets up to of an evening is far less psychologically detrimental than is the need felt by most narcissistically damaged individuals to lie to themselves and to the world about their false sense of inherent "badness". As we have seen, the process of developing psychic defences against rejection and loss begins in earliest childhood. Where emotional deprivation or abuse has occurred and the young person has attempted to "steal" and own the "badness" of the primary object in order to pretend that things are satisfactory, he or she will gradually invest tremendous psychic energy into protecting his or her emotional barricades, for fear of being discovered as fraudulent.

The most difficult element of secrecy here is that it often occurs on an unconscious level and is therefore tricky to decipher. When self-destructive behaviours are used to express underlying rage and grief, the behaviour itself can often remain secret for some time. Although some individuals who develop eating disorders or engage in self-harm have employed such behaviour primarily for attention, many others are conflicted about revealing their pain. Thus, for these latter individuals, the sense of shame they feel about these allegedly socially unacceptable behaviours and the difficult feelings they represent often prevents them from asking for help in the first instance. In addition, young people who are wounded by loss and separation are understandably wary of trusting and opening up to others.

Clinical implications

Clearly, adolescents who express their distress through self-destructive behaviour raise anxieties in the adults around them. In cases where parental involvement is minimal or abusive, young people may find it easier to reveal or hint at the use of self-destructive coping mechanisms at school or to other professionals with whom they are involved outside the home. Thus, teaching staff are often the first adults to be made aware of a young person's struggles with eating disorders or self-harm. In some respects this can be seen as a complimentary gesture, as it suggests that the adolescent trusts the educational professional enough to ask for help, however indirectly this might be conveyed at first. At the same time it can feel a terrible burden to bear for the adult, particularly if he or she is responsible for numerous other pupils as well.

The purpose behind including statistical information about eating disorders and self-harm as well as theoretical information about child and adolescent emotional development in this chapter is to highlight the fact that all adolescents have a great deal to contend with, and it is not unusual for many young people to express their rage through self-destruction. Of course, the key here is the degree to which the behaviour is being used and the extent to which it is interfering with and threatening the individual's development. It should also be noted that self-destructive behaviour can take on competitive and trend-setting qualities, particularly in the adolescent female population. Thus it is imperative for any adults involved to try and clarify the extent to which an individual's self-destructive behaviour is purely attention-seeking as opposed to being more symbolic of underlying distress.

As we have seen, where emotional abuse and/or deprivation has occurred and an adolescent has become narcissistically disturbed, he or she will crave emotional connection while at the same time attempting to deny this craving. A young person who has indicated a need for help on some level—be it physically or verbally—is more likely to respond positively to care, concern, and the opportunity to be heard. For individuals who appear responsive to intervention and who are not in any physical danger, counselling sessions in school and/or regular weekly meetings with a trusted member of staff, where the intention is to help them to learn to put feelings into words rather than actions, can be very successful. Although the behaviour may not disappear immediately, the importance of making an emotional connection with these young people, even if it is only once a week, should not be underestimated.

For example, I began seeing a 15-year-old girl for once-weekly counselling sessions in school because she had become depressed and was cutting herself. She had confessed her distress to her form tutor, who suggested counselling, and she agreed. Initially she was self-conscious and reluctant to talk about herself. However, after a few weeks she began to trust me and eventually started to explore issues around rage that she had never previously discussed with anyone. After a couple of months she began to understand the powerful emotions behind her urges to cut, and after about six months she was able to stop cutting altogether.

Similarly, at a private outpatient clinic I have been working for the last year with a 16-year-old youth with anorexia. His eating disorder and occasional cutting served as his only form of rebellion against his parents and as an expression of his fear of becoming an adult. For six months he appeared compliant in our once-weekly sessions but was unable to maintain any weight gain that occurred. Finally he came to trust me enough to express his rage and grief in the sessions and was therefore able to learn that I could withstand his outbursts and not reject him, which is an experience he had not previously had in his life. This process seems to have liberated him, and he no longer cuts and is nearly at a healthy weight.

As mentioned previously, mental health as a concept exists on a continuum, and most of us experience different points on that continuum throughout our lives. Because self-destructive behaviour is a symbolic expression of an emotional problem, the severity of any one individual's behaviour is directly related to the extent of his or her emotional wounding. Self-destructive adolescents who have relatively solid personalities and have experienced some amount of care and support, whether it be from a family member or not, are more likely to respond positively to therapeutic intervention. Conversely, individuals who have been deeply emotionally traumatized and continue to live in damaging conditions are less likely to be able to use therapeutic support, as it will feel threatening. These young people usually need intensive support from a number of professionals, such as social workers, general practitioners, and adolescent and family therapy centres. Obviously in cases where a young person is felt to be at risk by teaching staff, child protection procedures should be followed according to legal guidelines.

Conclusions

Eating disorders and self-harm are not uncommon practices among adolescents. For some, dabbling in self-destructive behaviour can be a phase that is eventually outgrown. For others, if the emotional distress underlying the behaviour is particularly complex and deep-rooted, intensive therapeutic and perhaps medical intervention may be required. Fundamentally, self-destructive behaviour in adolescence is indicative of a certain degree of narcissistic wounding that has not healed due to the inability of a primary care-giver to help the young person to manage difficult emotions. In most cases there will have been a loss or total lack of emotional connection with the primary care-giver, which infuriates and devastates the individual in childhood. If this emotional trauma is not rectified, the feelings will come to be experienced as intolerable by the time the individual reaches adolescence and also has to cope with the many physical and emotional changes that occur naturally during this period. For some young people, self-destructive behaviours like eating disorders and self-harm serve a defensive purpose against having to be consciously aware of painful feelings and also eventually attracts attention.

The realization that a young person is harming themselves can be shocking and anxiety-provoking for adults working with them in a professional capacity, but it is important to not be side-tracked by the behaviour in itself. Although many self-destructive adolescents do endanger their lives, and some will unfortunately do themselves deadly or irreparable damage, most do not. It is important for the adult professionals working with these individuals to remember that for the most part such behaviour is symbolic of an underlying need to connect emotionally with an adult. By listening and taking time to unravel the emotional distress that underlies eating disorders and self-harm, adults who have responsibility for these young people can, on some level, begin to repair a fundamental process that had, for many reasons, not gone right with the original primary care-givers. What this requires, more than anything, is empathy and an ability to separate one's own anxiety from that of the adolescent in question.

CHAPTER TWO

Beyond "bullies" and "victims": a systemic approach to tackling school bullying

Lucia Berdondini & Andreas P. D. Liefooghe

B ullying has received a great deal of attention over the past few decades. Ever since the groundbreaking work of Olweus (1977) in schools in Norway, the phenomenon of bullying has been researched internationally (e.g., among others, Berdondini & Genta, 2001; Genta, 2002; Smith & Myron-Wilson, 1998). This has not been restricted to schools: bullying at work (e.g. Einarsen, 1999; Liefooghe & Mackenzie Davey, 2001; among others) and bullying in communities (Randall, 1996) have also featured highly on the research agenda.

This chapter focuses on bullying in schools and draws on research from both developmental and organizational perspectives. After all, schools are organizations, and we believe that a lack of focus on the organization and system has led to seeking explanations for bullying purely at an individual level. Research typically examines characteristics of bullies and victims and offers explanations that draw on theories of, among others, aggression and personality. While we do not reject this research, we argue that over-individualizing distracts from a range of variables that can contribute to bullying incidents. In particular, in terms of interventions, a systemic perspective can provide a more balanced (and arguably more effective) way of dealing with bullying within schools.

Recent work by Twemlow (2000) presents an explanation of the bullying phenomenon and in particular of the Columbine High School massacre in Littleton, Colorado, from an integrated psycho-analytic approach (a combination of Adlerian, Stollerian, dialectical social systems, and Klein–Bion perspectives), arguing that several psychoanalytic models taken together converge to explain school violence and power struggles better than each does alone. In describing the anti-bullying intervention model that he and his colleagues applied in different schools, Twemlow mentions the systemic practical approach, which is similar to the one that is presented here.

In this chapter, we offer three case studies of school bullying. It is our aim to demonstrate that by working on the whole school system, bullying not only decreases but, in a parallel process, "bullies" as well as "victims" receive support. Young people who play a role in a bullying dynamic are not seen as carrying out harassing behaviours and abusing power at an individual level—instead, they are seen as one of the multiple elements of a unique system that both creates and feeds the bullying process. In particular, we want to highlight how other systems such as the family play a crucial role when considering school bullying behaviours. The cases presented here are drawn from a large-scale European anti-bullying project (Berdondini & Smith, 1996) that employs a variety of integrated prevention and intervention methods.

The influence of family background on bullying behaviour

Family background is considered a contextual influence on bullying dynamics. For instance, Smith and Myron-Wilson (1998) have reviewed studies in Europe, Australia, and the United States that have linked parenting and different roles in school bullying. Violent behaviour and harsh discipline by parents have been found to be connected to bullying behaviour, and over-protectiveness to being victimized. The links are complex, but a particularly interesting aspect of these studies is the axes of gender and dysfunctional parenting.

Bion (1967, pp. 103–104, 116) explains that the reverie of the mother is a quasi-therapeutic act of containment of fear and terror that ameliorates and transforms catastrophe. When the mother is unable to contain this terror, she rejects her child's attempts to communicate through projective identification, which makes the baby's experience meaningless. This is similar to the dread that affects both the perpetrator and the victim of violence. In the individual psychopathologies of violent people and of victims, it is likely that the maternal reverie was either absent or inadequate (Bion, 1967).

Schwartz, Dodge, Pettit, and Bates (1997) studied the early family experiences of boys who later emerged as aggressive victims, passive victims, non-victimized aggressors, and normative boys. The aggressive-victim group had experienced more punitive, hostile, and abusive family treatment than had the other groups, the non-victimized aggressive group, on the other hand, had a history of greater exposure to adult aggression and conflict, but not victimization by adults, than did the normative group. The passive victim group did not differ from the normative group on any home environment variable.

Among preadolescents there may be gender-specific links between perceived family interaction and peer victimization (Finnegan, Hodges, & Perry, 1998). For boys, victimization was associated with perceived maternal over-protectiveness, especially when boys reported reacting with fear during mother–child conflict. For girls, victimization was associated with perceived maternal rejection and with girls' reports of aggressive coping during mother–child conflict.

Rigby (1993) found that self-reported bullying correlated with poorer family functioning. Moreover, bullies reported poor relationships with fathers (boy bullies reported the same also with mothers), whereas among victims only data concerning girls were found significant: female victims reported poor relationships with mothers, but not with fathers.

Bowers, Smith, and Binney (1994) compared subgroups of bullies, victims, and bully/victims—also called "provocative victims": children who both bully and are bullied themselves—with uninvolved children, in their representation of family structure using the FAST, a projective test for representing emotional bonds (cohesion) and hierarchical structures in the family and similar social systems (Gehring, Debry, & Smith, 2001; Gehring & Wyler, 1986). They found that in bullies the family, particularly the parental dyad, is often represented as a disintegrated group, and that often the biological father is absent from home; the bullies usually perceived fathers as more powerful than mothers and themselves as less powerful within the family. Victims, by contrast, perceived the family as a close and united group; they tended to have more powerful fathers than mothers, but they did not perceive siblings and others family members as particularly powerful. Bully/victim children did not have cohesion scores as low as bullies but were similar to them in relegating some family members from the rest of the group. Again, the father was seen as particularly powerful compared to the mother. Bully/victims tended to have the highest power scores for self. Finally, uninvolved children showed a representation of their family as moderately cohesive and with father and mother quite powerful but with near equality between them.

Many of these findings were replicated in Italy by Berdondini and Smith (1996). In this study, only bullies, victims, and uninvolved children participated. The results showed, once again, that bullies often had no biological father at home. They also often represented their family with low cohesion, especially within the mother–father dyad. Again, results indicate a far more united family in victims.

Beyond categories

It is, of course, very important to explore possible links that relate individuals and family backgrounds to particular behaviours. Yet, when working with bullying in practice, it is equally important not to be too influenced by labels, roles, and categories. We should not forget that these labels are (a) imposed by observers, and are (b) at times too simplistic to describe a complex phenomenon. The cases outlined in this chapter fit some of the results described above in terms of family cohesion and environment, but they also present some elements that are not so coherent with the literature. For example, in two of the cases parental care did not appear to be at all violent or abusive.

Assuming that there are "bullying" and "victimized" children can be confusing when tackling a phenomenon of aggression in school. Children *are not* bullies or victims in the same way as they *are* blond or brown. Children *have* bullying or passive behaviours that make them *act* the role of bully or victim within a group. This is very different. Surely, officially identifying the person with a behaviour can produce a radicalization of that behaviour and gradually serve to reinforce that role.

Adler's (1958) group theory seems particularly useful in explaining exclusionary processes occurring within social groups. He argues that all individuals have a right to membership of a group and should not have to seek or earn this. Thus, the group, in excluding others, may engender narcissistic pathology in the individual excluded, who may avoid the group (victim) or force entry into it (bully).

Many studies have detailed the role-dependent way in which the bully interacts with the victim, influenced by the socially and personally defined roles of others in the surrounding environment (Twemlow, 1995a, 1995b; Twemlow, Sacco, & Williams, 1999). Moreover, Twemlow (1995a, 1995b) explained how the complex dialectical interaction between victim and victimizer is fuelled by the bystanders:

> Like cofactors in a chemical equation, the participants can influence the direction of the equation. The bully—victim—bystander relationship can be analogized to a mass law equation, with the bystander being the cofactor driving the relationship in either direction. [Twemlow, 2000]

In fact, bullying comprises a complex series of behaviours that encompasses not only those who are considered "bullies" and those who are perceived as "victims". It is a social phenomenon (Berdondini, Fantacci, & Genta, submitted; Liefooghe, 2001; Salmivalli, Lagerspetz, Bjorkqvist, Osterman, & Kaukiainen, 1996; Sutton & Smith, 1999), a relational process occurring within a group of persons who share time and experiences together and who perceive and experience the same dynamics in different ways.

In most bullying cases observed even in primary schools (Pepler & Craig, 1995), it was found that there was a group of bystanders who laughed and supported the bully or just watched and failed to intervene by helping the victim. In this way, they became responsible for reinforcing the phenomenon and the hierarchic roles. Recently, several studies explored the different possible roles of the bystanders in this type of social dynamic, discovering a variety of roles played by those apparently not directly involved in the phenomenon, such as "reinforcer" of the bully, "assistant" of the bully, "defender" of the victim, and "outsider" (Salmivalli et al., 1996; Sutton & Smith, 1999).

In a different group, or in the same group with a different atmosphere, the behaviours and consequently the roles of the same people may change. It is quite evident that the "bullies" exist only while the group allows them to play that role. Evidence (Salmivalli et al., 1996) suggests that even if only some of the bystanders intervene immediately to support the victim, the phenomenon of bullying could change significantly.

The same person can play different roles in different contexts: an assumption that is the cornerstone of work that aims to tackle bullying at school. In other words, the intervention is to reinforce positive alternative relational strategies and behaviours, more pro-social and cooperative to those that all pupils, bullies, bystanders, and sometimes even victims are used to. This assumes that everyone has the potential to access and become accustomed to positive social behaviour.

The anti-bullying project

The cases described in this chapter are drawn from an anti-bullying intervention project, funded by the cities of Bologna and Verrara and the University of Bologna (Berdondini, Fantacci, & Genta, submitted) and implemented in five Italian high schools. These are technical institutes where—alongside theoretical subjects, such as literature, history, mathematics, science, and foreign languages—students learn the technical aspects of a variety of jobs (graphic designer, electrician, plumber, and so on). A very large number of the pupils had been expelled from other establishments for anti-social behaviour (in Italy, school attendance is obligatory up to the age of 16). Other students are simply not interested in study and selected this school for its practical leaning. Nearly all of them tend to be from poor and deprived families, where it may be crucial for them to earn a living as early as possible. Perhaps because of this lack of motivation, there is a particularly high level of bullying: 42% of students reported frequent and serious incidents (Genta, 2002). An initiative to prevent bullying was essential.

Another characteristic typical of these schools is the level of stress faced by the teaching staff. With a difficult student group and sometimes threatened and attacked themselves, many teachers develop a somewhat detached attitude towards the class—and even towards their colleagues. Therefore, at the beginning of this project, it was likely to find teachers who:

- tried to teach the curriculum during lessons but avoided estab-lishing relationships with students and their families;
- were ultra strict with the class—even going as far as punishing and humiliating them as if to create a "climate of terror" that would enable them to maintain control;
- "turned a blind eye" to episodes of bullying;
- shunned those colleagues who tried to boost their students' motivation and behaviour;
- were dismissive of initial attempts at classroom interventions—often in front of students and at the expense of colleagues and members of the project team.

From a systemic perspective, one could argue that some of these teachers had adopted the role of bystanders, while others were clearly using bullying behaviour towards their own colleagues—sometimes tacitly encouraging their students to do the same. Indeed, there was a particularly aggressive—even violent—atmosphere in the classes that these people taught. Students would adopt attitudes similar to those of their teachers, excluding and rejecting both bullying and victimized peers. This situation existed in all three cases described in this chapter: the class and some teachers "watched" aggressive behaviour and did nothing.

This meant that, at first, only a few teachers in each school participated in the project and set about tackling the many difficul-ties—including their own colleagues' derision and resistance. Over time, as the results of the project became more evident (and head teachers continuing to offer training and supervision), more teachers participated and took part in training courses and applying intervention strategies. Now, only a few teachers have refused to be involved.

The project focuses not only on the individuals with obvious social problems but on the whole class. It tackles the "social climate" and works on building trust, improving communication, and fostering an atmosphere of social inclusion. From a systemic perspective, teachers are part of the group: as their role has a vital educational function, they are potentially critical in effecting change within the social dynamic. Taking the whole school (students *and* staff) as a system, bullying can occur between any members of that system—including teacher bullying student or teacher bullying teacher.

Within this project, teachers receive two or three months' training. The main approaches employed are drawn from *gestalt* therapy but also from other orientations, including psychodynamic, psychodrama, and occupational psychology. The teachers' training consists of weekly practical group sessions on the following.

- *theoretical introduction:* research in and studies on bullying; teachers' perceptions and definitions of bullying; the roles of bully, victim, and bystander; the power of the group;
- *facilitating class communication:* active listening, conflict resolution, peer support, problem-solving;
- *cooperative group work:* facilitating the class to work in groups;
- *enhancing self-awareness, dialogue and personal responsibility;*
- *practical strategies:* improving relationships between school and families; problem-solving with parents;.
- *peer support for teachers.*

The aim of the programme is to provide teachers with practical strategies, using cooperative activities to help pupils with their difficulties with relationships. More specifically, it focuses on quality of communication both with the class and with parents. Finally, through training and group supervision, the programme establishes peer support for staff that—drawing on a common "philosophy"—addresses the problem of bullying. Once trained, teachers start to implement these strategies, integrating them with the National Curriculum and often introducing group rather than individual work. In two of the colleges, teachers were also trained in counselling skills in order to offer a higher level of support. They also attend regular process groups and supervision, where they can present challenging cases and situations, share ideas, give and receive peer support, and explore their own emotional responses.

Wherever possible, parents are included in the project, attending parent/teacher meetings where they, too, receive training in anti-bullying strategies and communication skills. The key aim is to provide information and practical suggestions within a forum where parents can share their experiences, receive support, and also become part of the overall project. This effort to boost communication and cooperation between family and school is considered fundamental to the students' education.

Intervention programmes

Our research has indicated that bullying incidents are highly individual to each group. They can be direct (verbal or physical) or indirect (using social exclusion, for example); there can be one bully or victim or several; and so on. For each case, it is important to develop the most effective intervention. The factors that influence this include the characteristics of the class and the skills of the teachers. Teachers must believe that an intervention is workable—and will allow them to fulfil their teaching requirements.

Interventions fall broadly into two groups. The first is the introduction of specific techniques (including role play, group discussion, the "hot chair", trust-building exercises, and guided imagery). This involves the class in an explicit discussion of bullying in their class and an exploration of their own experiences.

However, this "head-on" approach is not appropriate in classes where students might feel blamed and rejected or where they could scapegoat one class member. In such situations, teachers can decide to tackle the situation through normal day-to-day activities but with an emphasis on group problem-solving and work. In this way, they can encourage a climate of trust and collaboration in which it becomes progressively safer to focus on more personal issues. What is critical for the success of this approach is to ensure that each person has a specific role or responsibility within a culture of respect.

With both interventions, the teacher will spend the last 10 to 15 minutes of the lesson de-briefing, facilitating discussion of the *group process* rather than of the activity itself.

Three of the five schools provided students with an opportunity to receive one-to-one counselling from trained teaching and non-teaching staff, thus integrating individual and group support.

It is interesting that when teachers first present a case of bullying, they generally identify it with a single student or a small group—the more overt "troublemakers". Later, when analysing the situation, they start to see how those individuals are only a part of a bigger picture in which everyone in the class plays an active and specific role. We present the following three cases as they were initially presented by the teachers, focusing on a single student.

Case studies

"Tamara"

Aged 16, Tamara is often described as a bully. She appears aggressive, insensitive, and lacking empathy. Since her mother died some years ago, her father has appeared depressed, working long hours and losing interest in his children's education and in running the house. Tamara is responsible for most domestic tasks—cooking, washing, and ironing—and she feels that without her the family would collapse.

She attends (regularly) the same school as her younger brother, who is a victim of bullying. He appears to express Tamara's sadness and tearfulness, which she keeps tightly under control. Instead, she is both physically and verbally aggressive with her fellow students. She focuses her taunts and denigration on a particularly group and has spread rumours about them and even destroyed some of their possessions in a fit of anger. She generally responds angrily to her classmates, who are intimi-

dated by and rejecting of her. When teachers punish or remon-
strate with her, she shows no emotions and often merely laughs.
Interestingly, her academic results are good.

What did we do?

Having consulted with teachers and governors at the school, we
conducted a training programme for teaching and non-teaching
staff in communication skills, active listening, student support, and
techniques to facilitate cooperative group work. We helped them to
shift their teaching style from "authoritative" to cooperative. In this
way they were able to address the difficulties in relating in the class
by encouraging in *all* students an awareness of and responsibility
for group dynamics. They also received monthly supervision sessions. The overall focus was on the culture in the classroom, not on
Tamara.

During the initial planning stages it emerged that Tamara, too,
was the victim of an indirect form of bullying and was excluded
and called names. We helped the teachers—in their class discussions—to draw attention to the atmosphere of "social exclusion"
that existed and to explore with their students class behaviour both
in and out of class. This allowed the young people to express their
confusion and feelings about others' actions and to clarify specific
incidents with those involved. This strategy was also introduced in
Tamara's brother's class, with the aim of supporting him, helping
him become less dependent on her, and integrating him with his
peers.

This project is still under way, but results over eight months
indicate a dramatic improvement in Tamara's attitude and behaviour, but also in all class relationships.

"Marco"

Marco is 17 years old and is an only child. He is intelligent and
consistently achieves good marks. His father is an academic, his
mother a high-school teacher. He was brought to our attention
because of his "aggressive and provocative attitude towards
teaching staff" and his lack of respect for authority. He is,
however, popular with peers and uses this to lead a group in

severe forms of bullying towards other classmates. They focus in particular on one girl, whom they covered with spit. They also victimize a boy and have urinated in his shoes during PE, spread vicious rumours, called him names, and stolen from him. They have even threatened him with a knife (the only example of direct intimidation). It was when this boy reported the incident to his parents that the episode was brought to the attention of the teaching staff.

The school immediately contacted Marco's parents. They appeared very distressed and were completely unaware of their son's aggressive behaviour at school. They described him as a "model" child: sociable, gentle, considerate, and with many friends. Marco's parents were in favour of severe sanctions and said that they were going to take him seriously in hand. However, at this point there was little change in his behaviour (although he never brought a knife to school again). He continued to bully the boy indirectly and the girl both physically and psychologically.

What did we do?

In this instance, we felt that it was important to involve the parents. We trained teaching and non-teaching staff in techniques that they could introduce into the classroom to address bullying. We also conducted a communication skills course for parents (in which Marco's mother and father participated enthusiastically). This developed into a "peer-support group" where parents could meet regularly to discuss issues relating to their children.

By coincidence, we were working on an anti-bullying video project (funded by the University of Bologna and the city of Ferrara). This was being filmed in various high schools and would be used as teaching material. We decided to involve Marco's class in this project—actually filming students involved in role play, "hot chair", communication exercises, and problem-solving activities. At the same time we aimed to help them become more aware of their own behaviour and attitudes.

We showed the class some filmed interviews with victims in which they expressed their humiliation, rage, and fear—which often extended beyond school to other areas of life. These clips could often be quite brutal, with young people confessing to thoughts of suicide or of fantasies of "massacring" their classmates.

We interview Marco and his peers several times about their reactions to the videos. Marco proved himself to be articulate and thoughtful, trying to explain why bullying happens and describe his own perceptions of the victims' experiences. In fact, he proved to be insightful and honest and admitted that he himself had been responsible for bullying incidents—blaming boredom—but had never before considered the impact his actions might have had on others, as he considered what he was doing merely a "joke". He acknowledged that he had been quite disturbed by the interviews with victims in the video.

Following this exercise, teachers noticed a change in Marco's behaviour. His victims, who were being given one-to-one support by teachers, also remarked on a difference in the way he acted towards them. The class itself also changed, with pupils becoming equipped to tackle interpersonal problems through classroom discussion.

"Pierre"

At 14, Pierre is the elder of two sons of recently divorced professional parents. He is intelligent but does not do well at school and is notorious for his disruptive behaviour. He appears to have no sense of right and wrong, reacting violently to the least perceived provocation. He has broken furniture and assaulted both peers and staff and been suspended many times. However, nothing has had an impact on his aggression.

Some teachers reacted to him in a disparaging and dismissive way in front of his peers. At first they refused to become involved with the project but later changed their minds. The parents were highly cooperative and wanted to work with the school. Indeed, they had sent Pierre for external counselling to help him cope with the difficulties they felt were associated with the break-up of their marriage.

Pierre is a part of group—some of them from seriously troubled backgrounds: one has been in several foster homes, another is a drug-user, while a third was abused physically by this father—all of whom behave in a similar way. On the surface, Pierre's personal circumstances appear less problematic than those of his friends, yet he is the most aggressive.

What did we do?

One teacher (her colleagues refused to become involved) attempted to tackle Pierre and his friends' behaviour head-on. However, he retaliated by leaving the classroom, accusing her of scapegoating him. A more indirect intervention was felt to be more appropriate, and three teachers volunteered for training in cooperative group work.

The teacher who had tried to intervene communicated her own frustration at the response of the class and explained that while she was going to abandon any further attempts at open discussion, she felt it essential to work to improve the overall class culture. To this end, she introduced an increased level of group work. As a science teacher, she ensured that the students conducted all laboratory experiments in groups, with a focus on working together effectively. Towards the end of each class, she held a debriefing, encouraging students to consider how they had experienced collaborating in this way and how they would further "improve" the group process.

The class participated enthusiastically. Even Pierre and his friends were keen, and in the third group-focused lesson, asked the teacher to teach them about drugs. For the first time, they discussed their drug experiences openly and showed genuine curiosity about the chemical effects of their use. This session ended with an informal and open group discussion, with Pierre and his peers exploring their personal experiences of the advantages and disadvantages of drugs. The teacher paid particular attention to listening without judgement, commenting instead on their ability to share something of themselves with her and their classmates. For the first time, Pierre participated in a discussion without disrupting matters and seemed to take some pride in his contributions. In their feedback, his classmates reflected how positive it had been for them to see him behaving not aggressively, but in a communicative and supportive fashion. For his part, Pierre was both surprised and moved by their comments.

Throughout this process, the teacher met with his parents—sometimes on their own and sometimes with parents of other class members. She explained the aim of the programme, what was happening in the classroom, and the results that she had noticed. After a couple of months, Pierre's parents reported some improvement in his behaviour.

This teacher continues to use a cooperative approach with this group, asking students to present scientific issues—diet and nutrition, sport and steroids—that have some relevance in their private lives). Having seen her success, other teachers are implementing similar strategies in their own classrooms and have noted a marked improvement not only in Pierre's behaviour but also in the attitude of the whole class.

Conclusion

It is clear from these case studies that taking a "holistic" approach to dealing with bulling—including both systemic and contextual factors—provides deeper insight. By using teachers as "agents of change", bullying dynamics can often shift rapidly and dramatically. However, back-up—by peers and professionals—for these teachers is essential, as is a strategy underpinned by sound theory and evidence. Sadly, not everyone—either teachers or parents—will have similar resources on which they can draw, and there are a number of key points that should be stressed:

1. Bullying is not always easily identified. The term is used widely and there is often confusion about what constitutes a bullying incident. However, it can play a part in severe behaviours such as drug addiction at one end of the spectrum and, at the other end, what seem like innocuous episodes that are still highly stressful for the individual at the receiving end.

    The first steps in dealing with bullying is to raise awareness that people differ in their responses and that everyone needs to be responsible for his or her actions and the impact they have on others. Naturally, raising awareness of the issue results in an increase in reported incidents. However, it is vital that this does not act as an argument against tackling it. From our experience, whenever someone claims that he or she is being bullied (and in this chapter we have avoided offering a single definition of the phenomenon), there is something that warrants investigation.

2. There is evidence that young people with a history of emotional and behavioural disturbance are more likely than others to be either bullies or victims. Considering this fact early in the programme is important, as being "different" in some way is often enough for a group to target, reject, or exclude people.

3. While certain individuals (through their own aggressive behaviour or their scapegoating by others) become the most visible, we should not lose sight of the group and the wider context within which bullying occurs. At times, the group can express its hostility and tension and attempt to establish a hierarchy by targeting different individuals.

4. Working with the group does not preclude individual support—in fact, both need to work together. Support at an individual level needs to be in place alongside group-focused intervention strategies.

5. As far as possible, working with bullying should be incorporated into the curriculum. Adding "special" sessions on bullying creates the impression that it is an "optional extra" rather than a core issue.

6. There is no quick fix. While it is tempting to offer a "magic formula", the reality is that interventions are "messy" and idiosyncratic, depending on the variables such as teachers, students' problems, group composition, and the general social dynamic of the class.

7. Finally, anyone working on a bullying strategy should be prepared to get his or her hands dirty. However, as long as we look beyond the labels of "bully" and "victim" and avoid taking action hastily, a systemic approach has the potential to provide lasting change in "difficult" classrooms. At the same time, anyone involved in a

project should be open to using a wider, "integrative" toolbox. As Adler said:

Every human being strives for significance, but people always make mistakes if they do not see their whole significance must consist in the contribution to the lives of others. [Adler, 1958, p. xvi]

CHAPTER THREE

Parent battering and its roots in infantile trauma

Reinmar du Bois

C hildhood is filled with powerful emotions: fear, panic, uncertainty, excitement, powerlessness, rage, triumph, love, and hate. When these feelings are left uncontained—either by parents or in play—and if there has also been trauma, the child can be quite overwhelmed. His response may be increasingly violent behaviour.

Child-battering and "partner-battering" are both well documented. However, parent-battering has received little attention. This chapter focuses on the subject of parent-battering and argues that an overly traumatic primary relationship can result in an adolescent acting violently towards his parents.*

The causes of aggression

In both humans and animals, aggression is associated with neuronal activity in the limbic system (Eichelman, 1983). This controls

---

*Although parent battering is not confined exclusively to boys, in this chapter the male pronoun has been used, for ease of expression.

the "fight-or-flight" impulse and is where the origins of fear or an
aggressive impulse originate. Other areas of the brain (specifically,
the frontal cortex) are also involved in human aggressive behaviour (Mark & Irvine, 1970). Both neurological and psychological
research has shown that human aggression is not determined by
drives and cannot be likened to instinctual behaviour. While the
classic notion of a boiler with a valve to relieve mounting pressure
is too simplistic, there is solid biological evidence that aggression is
based on a strong, natural disposition and may vary according to
individual temperament and hormonal (testosterone and steroids)
influences.

That said, developmental factors—external and internal—are
also significant. It has been established that aggression follows
certain neuronal pathways that are laid down early in human
development (even before birth) by experiences and learning patterns.

As a child grows up, he gradually learns the social rules and
conventions that govern behaviour. This allows him to modify his
personal aggressive behaviour and even "revise" his aggressive
fantasies. Parents are no longer the target of his anger and rage.
However, throughout life, there is a precarious balance between the
internal, personal dynamics of aggression (which may be revealed
only to certain people) and the external aspects of aggression
(which relate to morality, attitudes, politics, and public behaviour).

Adler (1908) regarded aggression not as dangerous or destructive but as a creative, natural force that promoted autonomy and
willpower. Freud (1930a) insisted on aggression's potential for self-
destruction and argued that only repression and sublimation of
sexual and aggressive instincts lead to creativity and cultural
achievement. In modern theories of child development, the term
"aggression" often describes a behavioural style or internal motivation that becomes visible in states of excitement, in play or in
interaction with parents or peers. While these aspects of childhood
"aggression" may sometimes appear extreme, they are generally
far removed from actual violence. However, where they do im-
pinge on the real world and manifest as actual behaviour, the child
and/or his parents may be shattered.

The extent of a child's aggressive fantasy depends both on
whether parent–child interaction is avoidant or provocative, alien-

ating or familiarizing and on the child's innate receptivity and ego-stability. (Children with autistic traits tend to develop the most bizarre aggressive fantasies, which serve to stimulate them or fill the void left by a lack of social interaction and understanding.)

In early development, aggression usually has little symbolic significance. It may be directed towards the self or towards objects to which the baby eventually develops an attachment. Initially, aggression may be no more than an internal arousal; then, an intentional state leads to the search for an object. Finally, aggression is vested with symbolic meaning and becomes rooted in relationships. From a psychoanalytic perspective, it is impossible to conceive of an act of violence merely as an outpouring of aggression without an object. However, while the object of aggression may not be the same as the "victim" of the aggressive act, there will be some symbolic link that can be understood within the context of personal experience.

Infantile distress

Winnicott (1958) described the baby's intense crying as "relentless". His distress, even it is interpreted as a meaningful signal to the mother, takes into account neither his own emotional and physical resources nor his mother's capacity to endure his distress. It is "all or nothing". If this state continues for a long time, it is usually due to an unbalanced state of sympathetic autonomous functioning—or it can be interpreted as an indication of a state of emotional emergency.

The "meaning" of a baby's crying is open to interpretation. Contemporary research suggests that one infant's irritability differs markedly from that of another and does not predict later aggression (Thomas & Chess, 1977). A mother can be embarrassed by her inability to interpret whether her baby is crying because of anxiety, rage, pain, despair, or wilfulness. Whatever her interpretation—whether right or wrong—the child will pick up on it and reassess the situation accordingly. Gradually, the mother's reaction will define his perception of his own emotions.

Prenatal mechanisms of affect control are still dominant throughout the first three months of life. As the infant grows older, affect modulation relies increasingly on his motor and sensory activity combined with longer periods of wakefulness and the capacity to direct attention to activity and objects around him. His ability to regulate distress also depends on good, fast, and continual interaction between child and mother. This type of communication has been called symbiotic because the baby is unlikely to experience his mother as a separate being: in fact, the mother virtually synchronizes her own bodily perceptions with those of her child.

There is a clinically important group of conspicuously quiet and non-responsive babies. Throughout the first 12 months, for reasons that are as yet unknown, they ignore interactive ways of regulating mood and remain passive and generally inactive. As they enter the second year of life, some of them become hyperactive—possibly as a reaction to the high levels of stimuli that confront them as they start to walk. A purely neurophysiological explanation assumes that such a child has always been overwhelmed by excessive stimuli and that negative feedback mechanisms blocked his dopamine receptors during infancy. Maturational changes during the second year of life alter receptor functioning, with the effect that the sensory overload that had caused the "blockage" is now responsible for hyperactivity. Notwithstanding the dramatic change of motor activity, the toddler retains the poor stimulus and affect control that characterized his infancy.

This neurophysiological model appears to explain the onset of excessive childhood aggression. In reality, the complex dynamics have merely been translated into biological terms. The development of neuronal functioning and biochemical reaction patterns depend on communication and sensory stimulation. Therefore, it is hardly surprising that trauma can impair the maturation of brain function. Freud's later (1920g) theory that internal stimuli alone could overwhelm a particularly excitable infant and cause trauma is scarcely tenable in the light of modern empirical evidence. In order to suffer psychic trauma, even the most agitated infant must be deprived of the containment provided by normal maternal care and nursing activities.

Research into the impact of child neglect and abuse has defined clearly what causes trauma. The child may have been ignored or abandoned in a state of tension, upset, and need or been tormented and intimidated. He may have witnessed parental violence yet understood neither what was happening nor how he should respond (Cummings, Vogel, Cummings, & El Sheikh, 1988). Such experiences often fascinate and paralyse a small child; his response manifests—in essence—the symptoms of acute post-traumatic stress disorder. We must assume that even a very young child retains fragmented physical and situational memories of these events, which he later recalls. This traumatic material can be revived during adolescence. Furthermore, a lack of stable and protective relationships to buffer and contain the child's behaviour often increases the likelihood of an escalation of aggression.

Rough-and-tumble play illustrates how aggression can be contained in a way that allows the child to express and experience his aggression within the context of robust affect control, negotiation of appropriate boundaries, and maintenance of "good" contact with his playmates (Aldice, 1975; Boulton, 1994; Dugas, Mouren, & Halfon, 1985). Such play —initially between child and parents and later with peers—sits somewhere between harm and harmlessness. The child challenges his "opponents" and is later reconciled with them. Ideally, parents also teach him to interpret playmates' signals, to understand gestures and body language, to stop before things "turn nasty", and to settle conflicts.

Aggression and autonomy
from childhood to adolescence

A toddler's temper tantrums are closely related to adolescent crises. Such behaviour indicates that the child is failing to complete a self-imposed task and is unable to control his frustration. The aggression of a tantrum is partly directed towards the self and partly towards an attachment figure. It is often associated with omnipotent fantasies but can "slip" into a regressed state. Like rough-and-tumble play, it contains the wish for comfort and reconciliation but also evokes the fear that the "target" may suffer permanent injury or reject and abandon the "naughty" child. Each tantrum signifies a painful breakdown of the autonomy to which the child aspires and is suspended between omnipotence and powerlessness, independence and dependence.

An adolescent's rebelliousness revisits the themes of a toddler's tantrum. The early bids for autonomy have a strong developmental significance, providing the child with a sense of his capabilities as well as of his limitations, at first, he declines help, then he cries for it and is eventually forced to accept that sometimes there is no solution. In such situations, boundaries between parent and child can be clarified and reinforced.

Some children fail to display aggressive traits when they are toddlers and undergo such crises for the first time only when they reach adolescence. Other children experience these outbursts from a very young age. The delayed and continual expression of aggression indicates that there is a disturbance in the drive towards autonomy. Parents and children find themselves stuck within an ambivalent relationship in which there is no escape from the family conflict: in fact, any anger merely leads back to this aggression.

Where a family has negotiated such conflicts successfully, the child uses aggressive fantasy play to organize and manage his destructive impulses. Of course, it is quite possible that this playfulness can lead to an actual destructive act, and there are particular types of aggressive fantasy with a stereotypical content and persecutory quality that *do* lead to aggressive behaviour.

There are two complementary theories that explain the emergence of aggressive fantasies. Winnicott (1986) argues that aggressive impulses form the basic dynamic starting-point of all childhood experience: the child seeks to create emotional tension in order to resolve it and "renew" his sense of relief and comfort. Paradoxically, he wants to put his world at risk and then have the satisfaction of finding that it is intact. Michael Balint (1959) implies a similarly ambivalent mechanism in his suggestion that a child chooses the thrill of risk-taking and quasi-aggressive behaviour in order to reassure himself that by overcoming such dangers, he can regain the early experience of "primary love". At the same time, he is old enough to seek out more mature object relations that demand a degree of detachment from primary relationships.

In some typical aggressive childhood play, dolls or toys are mutilated or subjected to ruthless "surgery". In this way, the child's most treasured possession becomes the target for his "bad thoughts". The process of "magical thinking" keeps him in some doubt that this play may not become reality, and so he continually seeks reassurance from adults that his violent actions are really harmless and that no one is permanently injured. Freud would have argued that a child's constant struggle against his feelings of guilt arise from his aggressive drive. More recent theories see guilt as a basic human capacity parallel with, not secondary to, aggression.

Trauma theorists (Terr, 1991) assert that aggressive fantasies are fuelled by previous experiences of desertion, helplessness, lack of reassurance, pain, paralysis, anticipated or postponed threats of punishment, and loss of affect control. The duration and frequency of these experiences contribute to the level of trauma. A child who has been abused in this way over a long period will have aggressive fantasies and eventually resort to violent behaviour. This is the classical role reversal: from victim to aggressor (Burgess, 1987; A. Freud, 1936). However, it should be stressed that children who report aggressive fantasies are rarely victims of permanent physical harm. They are often from an unstable family background and closely allied to a weak, depressed mother who is abused by a male partner.

Parents are frequently paralysed by their child's increasingly aggressive behaviour—perhaps because what they perceive in their offspring is a reflection of their own distorted relationship with him. Where an infant behaves in this way, parents may fear losing their temper and responding with equal aggression. Thus, the desperation of both parents and child mounts and can end in physical punishment.

These situations share an over-controlled, underlying aggression, which is suppressed until it finally erupts. The key emotions are fearful anticipation, concealed panic, and inner tension, with a strong denial of any aggressive emotions or fantasies.

Battered-parent syndrome

As recently as the late 1970s, Steinmetz (1978) and Harbin and Madden (1979) described a type of children's violence towards their parents. Literature exploring this phenomenon remains limited and based entirely on case studies (Charles, 1986; Chartier & Chartier, 2002; Paulton & Coombes, 1990). Two major surveys undertaken in 1998 by Du Bois and his associates (Du Bois, 1998; Du Bois, Gaebele, & Schaal, 1987) and Jakob (1994) both revealed an incidence of between 60 and 70 such cases in the population of 9.5 million in Baden-Württemberg, in prosperous south Germany. The "perpetrators" ranged in age from 8 to 22, with a mean of 16.5 and an absolute peak at 14 in both sexes. There appeared to be a large number of unreported cases.

In this study, cases of battered-parent syndrome were characterized by regular physical abuse of the mother or the father, triggered by petty arguments. The abuse occurred over a minimum period of three months, and often much longer. Other characteristics included the parents' helplessness, failure to seek effective support, and strong feelings of shame and guilt. In 90% of the cases, the mothers were the victims; in the remaining 10%, *both* parents suffered. As well as abusing one or both parents, the child often behaved in a tyrannical manner and refused to attend school. Most cases were reported to social services or referred to child guidance centres or, occasionally, to a general practitioner.

General dynamic considerations

Everyone who has written about parent battering has raised doubts about whether or not it should be labelled a new syndrome. Despite the general overly aggressive behaviour towards the parents, there is a prevailing impression that the cases differed significantly from one another in many other respects. In our own survey, low-income families were over-represented. Both inside and outside this group, failure at school was four times higher than in the general population—even after excluding those cases with overt psychopathology that might contribute to poor academic performance.

Of the affected families, 37% appeared to be socially isolated. This group correlated with that of parents over the age of 35 at the time of the birth of the affected child (25%). Of the children (80% male, 20% female), 22% showed signs of emotional disturbance in addition to violence; these included eating disorders, compulsive disorder, autistic traits, depression, and phobias. Alcohol and substance abuse was present in a further 15%. Only 9% had had previous contact with a psychiatric service, and no child was considered to be disturbed enough to warrant mandatory in-patient treatment. In all other cases, mental and emotional functioning appeared satisfactory. However, 36% had already manifested anti-social tendencies and been involved in petty crime. About 75% of all cases of battered-parent syndrome could be characterized by at least one of three clusters of risk factors—emotional, intellectual, or social. More disturbingly, about a quarter of all cases remained unexplained.

While these findings confirm patterns of aggressive behaviour towards parents, they do not support the idea of a uniform and clearly defined syndrome—more of a loose group of cases of considerable heterogeneity. To find a "common denominator" for parent battering, we conducted extensive qualitative research. The aim was to define an area of overlap in the approaches to understanding the underlying mechanisms. Several "causes" were inconclusive. These included "poorly educated parents" (evident in a lack of rules, values and a positive father figure) and "overt psychopathology" in parent or child. However, there was a strong consensus that "distorted early parent–child interaction" was a fruitful area for exploration in considering the dynamics of parent-battering. This conclusion was supported by:

1. observation of both over-protectiveness and ambivalence towards the child by one or both parents;

2. dependent, passive and symbiotic tendencies towards the child;

3. an almost masochistic attitude towards being beaten by one's child;

4. an indication that some of the children may have been abused;

5. a strong indication that "contact disorders" (see below) were even more common among members of affected families than could be guessed from the fact of obvious social isolation

Regressive arousal states

"Distorted parent–child interactions" can best be illustrated by the battering scenes themselves, which are reminiscent of primitive arousal states in very young children. The violence appears like a compulsion to repeat infantile abreaction to inner tension. Perpetrator and victim are held together by overwhelming helplessness and neediness. The recognition of this creates more uneasiness, which leads to further aggression. The adolescent behaves destructively, with mother watching his behaviour. Even the parent may be manhandled as if she were merely a toy or transitional object. The adolescent may even cry loudly as he beats his parents.

The whole situation is often desperate for both parent and child. When you consider the sometimes fragile container that parents must provide for an upset, frightened, and angry child and how easily the child introjects his parents' undigested aggression, it is unsurprising that adolescents can still be entangled in an aggressive dynamic—except now the parent is the victim.

A 20-year-old who presented quite normally outside the family home charged at his mother and "punished" her because he had a nose-bleed. A 14-year-old often left the house, ignoring his parents' pleas, then got drunk before coming home. His father and mother would be sitting on the sofa, as if waiting for him to physically abuse them. Sometimes the boy would fall asleep in the middle of a violent episode; his mother would then cover him with a blanket and stroke his head. The abuse resumed when he woke.

Most adolescents who batter their parents foster a strong hatred for their mother: after all, she remains the all-important trigger for a violent outburst. An adolescent often threatens his mother using the same words and tone of voice he used in infancy. Despite the level of aggression, the language that accompanies attacks is often apologetic or expressive of a wish to surrender—which may explain why so many women who are battered by their child dismiss the real danger that faces them and fail to protect themselves. The behaviour reminds them of a toddler's temper tantrum. Thus, even if a mother sustains severe injuries, she may still imagine that she is in control—a fantasy that is interrupted only by a further horrific outburst.

Contact disorders

From a clinical and practical viewpoint one may describe "contact disorder" as a group of personality traits that contribute to the formation of and inability to resolve distorted relationship patterns between parent and child. "Contact disorders" are manifested by lacking tolerance, competence, interest, and alertness in all areas of social intercourse and a general paucity of social activities outside the inner family circle. The underlying temperamental traits range from "introvert" to "odd–eccentric" and "autistic-like" and may be traced back to disturbed early interactions, poor social emotional perception of the infant, maternal depression, deprivation, or early trauma.

Parent battering manifests itself at a time when children are expected to separate from their parents to lead their own lives. For most adolescents, steady developmental progress is generally made with additional support from school, peer groups, the local community, and other social networks. All sorts of experiences and relationships attract them away from their family into the wider world, with their own intellectual growth supporting them in this distancing. Furthermore, within this process, they manage to contain feelings of anger and aggression.

Adolescents often avoid spending too much time with their parents so as not to be confronted with the vestiges of their earlier emotional dependency. They may also be embarrassed to discover how aggressive and sexual feelings are somewhat linked and may want to avoid displaying such "passion" in a way that will affect their parents.

Typical parent-battering behaviour only happens when personal growth and social support are disrupted or absent. Parents with contact disorders may be unable to transfer personal conflict away from their primary relationships. It is assumed that such disorders induce people to cling to primary love objects (Balint, 1968) as the external world retains an aura of danger, "strangeness", and inaccessibility. Similarly, such parents could overlook the fact that their child is striving for autonomy and—again—contribute to the development of "parent-battering pathology". A mother's indication that her child's separation from her is causing anxiety signals that she is weak and dependent and may have an unsettling effect on the adolescent. On the other hand, the mother may try to avoid confrontation and rejection by accepting bad behaviour and treatment. Unconsciously, she may hope that he is affected by a sense of guilt that unites him with her and the father and contribute to what is, in effect, sado-masochistic collusion.

For research purposes we had to modify our dynamic concept of "contact disorder" and attempt a definition based on three empirically established concepts in social psychology:

1. *"lack of social competence"*:   an inability to behave appropriately in anxiety-provoking situations; intense anxiety in some situations; failure to recognize both one's own needs and those of others;

2. *"attachment deficiency"*:   a lack of integration with one's peer group, coupled with the experience of being unpopular and rejected and lacking empathic relationships;

3. *"poor social integration"*:   an inability to integrate into a social framework (school, work, sports and leisure clubs, etc.).

Using a semi-structured questionnaire, we conducted a series of telephone interviews with agencies and colleagues who had reported cases of parent battering. We also sent to the parents and children of affected families a structured questionnaire designed to assess contact disorder. While we only received 30 responses from this group (out of a total of 70), results confirm convincingly a high incidence of contact disorders in both parents and the affected children. In a smaller number of responses, only the parents exhibited symptoms of contact disorder.

Critical appraisal of contemporary family structures

Even though we may feel that developmental experiences and temperamental factors are responsible for contact disorders within parents and their children, it is worth assessing recent social and cultural changes that may have influenced family structure. Young people today need a relatively high degree of autonomy and ego-stability in order to move into modern society—with all its options, opportunities, and challenges—without apprehension or fear . . . and without being manipulated by media and fashion to a point where they lose touch with reality.

On starting work, it is unusual for an adolescent to have a meaningful vocational career to help him to establish a stable sense of identity. There is also the risk that he may be forced to leave (or avoid) family life before achieving a strong sense of social integration. This can lead him to turn to the nearest "intimate" refuge— becoming a parent within a family of his own—before he is ready for such responsibility or to a peer group that exerts a strong "pull" to regress—perhaps through alcohol or drugs.

Modern family structures are vulnerable. Parents and children form close but ambivalent ties and neglect the challenge of integration into a wider social milieu. An adolescent may try to free himself from these exclusive family ties but then experience such attempts as frustrating and ineffective.

Paradoxically, society sets a high degree of autonomy as a norm, which can result in considerable conflict. The family strives for a high level of intimacy, warmth, and security in an attempt to protect itself from a world perceived as impenetrable and hostile. It will consider the task of nursing a young baby as one that is best managed by offering the infant exclusive attention. This may be undertaken in isolation, and the parents surrender themselves to a kind of solitary confinement. The mother may even expect to receive warmth and intimacy from her baby, with the result that— as the child gets older—mutual disappointment and recrimination are unavoidable. Thus, the parents find that family life fails to offer the gratification and meaning for which they had hoped—and which they had promised their child.

From a sociological perspective, this "constellation" of false promises, in conjunction with a disappointing and frustrating reality, is an important trigger for the child's rage towards his parents. Once that child reaches adolescence, the gap between social demands and the personal capacity for autonomy widens. Since infancy, love, and hate have been incompatible and have been directed alternately towards the same people.

During childhood, it is possible to gloss over poor social relationships: parents and school life maintain only limited social interaction. However, on leaving school and starting work or further education, an ability to "fake" autonomy is not enough. The young person is prey to social discomfort, frustration, and rejection and then retires into his family, where he starts to behave in a regressed manner and can virtually take his parents hostage. He withdraws from work or education and gradually restricts his range of social activity until only the family remains.

Therapeutic interventions

It is rare for a psychotherapeutic intervention to be used at this stage. Those cases that can be explored in greater depth—generally those involving forcible inpatient treatment of a severely withdrawn adolescent or a strong working alliance between therapist and parents—reveal a history of a younger child being kept in a similar but more subtle "hostage situation", which, at the time, was not visible to observers.

Treatment for parent battering is not psychotherapy in the conventional sense. First, it is unusual for any family member to be prepared to accept such help. Furthermore, the young person vehemently opposes any attention or involvement from outside the family and may prevent his parents from contacting external agencies. Such a move, in his eyes, is total betrayal. Parents who have the courage to seek help have taken an important step towards the resolution of abnormal patterns of relating that fulfil the criteria for sado-masochistic collusion.

Sometimes, the parents manage to escape from their child or even throw him out of their home. The frequent response to such a move is delinquency. Ultimately, such a dramatic response fails to end the parent–child entanglement but serves, instead, to embarrass and trap the parents still further. Delinquent acts represent retaliation against the parents and may be preceded by repeated— and unsuccessful—demands for money. Some young people who are caught and receive a custodial sentence appear strangely cheerful. An emotional exploration indicates that, imprisoned, they nurture strong fantasies of punishing their parents and indulging their imagined sadistic powers.

Any agency that offers support to the parents provides some form of therapeutic help. The first step is always the parents' decision to disclose their plight to an external authority. Social services are often the first port of call, but even the police can initiate a dialogue with parents and help to introduce new rules that benefit the family. Above all, parents need encouragement to "come out of hiding", move forward, and seek new allies *external* to the family.

Case vignette: "S.S."

S.S. was a 14-year-old boy of average intelligence. His parents came to me without their son and insisted that I should keep their consultation strictly confidential. They were concerned about their neighbourhood and their relatives, but above all they were frightened that visit to a psychiatrist might be disclosed to their son. He had often threatened that he would "punish" them if they involved anyone external to the family. The parents' report about their son was a quaint mixture of agonizing confession and educational shop talk. Both were teachers and stressed that they were intellectually superior to this young man, as were their elder son and their younger daughter. He had become peripherally involved in the local skinhead scene "to boost his self-confidence"—and demanded that his parents buy him the entire subculture outfit, including weaponry (!).

The parents engaged in absurd reasoning as to the extent of their leniency and how worried they should be about their child's emotional turmoil. The father indulged in memories of a particular emotional closeness between himself and this son when he was still an "innocent" child. At the same time, however, both parents appeared cool and arrogant. It was then disclosed that when the boy was alone with his mother, he would dog her footsteps, and that he had often kicked her shins and threatened her with a knife. The first therapeutic intervention was to empower the parents to resist their son without being overwhelmed by aggressive impulses or guilt feelings.

At the next session, the parents reported triumphantly that they had reprimanded their son, and he had then withdrawn to his room. His obsessive behaviour had worsened. It was obvious that the roles of omnipotence and powerlessness had just reversed. The parents took several more sessions to untangle and reconcile the convoluted elements of their own hatred, guilt (for lack of love for this particular son), marital conflicts, and feelings of dependency on the grandparents. A turning point was reached when the parents managed to reveal to their son that they were receiving therapeutic counselling. Still, he was not prepared to accept that he needed help himself.

It was decided that all future help directed towards the boy should be kept strictly separate from the help being given to the parents. It then became known that he had been involved in gang fights, and criminal proceedings were imminent. The father rushed to the lawyer's office and claimed that his son was too young, disturbed, and immature to be taken to court. Much persuasion was needed to convince the father that he should not interfere and acknowledge realistic boundaries between his parental role and the impact of the outside world. I was relieved to see that the police acted as a third party, which was able to "triangulate" with the boy and his parents.

It is always the parents who take the first step to free themselves from their role as victim; then the adolescent is forced to risk changing himself. Any therapeutic approach to parent battering must include an element of social management combined with fostering in-depth understanding of the vicious circle of behaviour in which the family is imprisoned. It is important to "accompany" the parents as they undergo a process of separation from their child and then undertake a phase of personal maturation. Following the first essential goal of physical separation, the parents feel intensely disoriented and guilty—and now accept psychotherapy readily. By contrast, the young person is often helped by being in new circumstances to which he may well adapt surprisingly quickly.

That said, it is important not to underestimate the persistence of sado-masochistic collusion. A 17-year-old girl had received extensive inpatient psychotherapy following aggressive behaviour towards her mother and had finally agreed to attend university in another town. Three years later, she returned home temporarily while looking for a job. There followed a major return to violent patterns of behaviour: an argument developed into a perverse scene in which the girl flogged her mother with a garden hose.

CHAPTER FOUR

Violence in care

Bruce Irvine

Being in care

> I don't want to talk about it
> I DON'T WANT TO TALK ABOUT IT
> I don't want to say anything
> Thinking about it hurts me HURTS ME
>
> *Hitchum, aged 10* (VCC, 1998)

B eing in care, being "Looked After" is a complicated, difficult, and often painful process. When a child is placed in the
care of the local authority, the process is often acrimonious
and difficult, the experience for the child traumatic, and the experience of professionals working in the area often soul-destroying.
The intensity of the crisis that precipitates the child into being
removed from their family underlies the exposure of a fundamentally important anxiety on behalf of society. The child being received into care is ultimately the result of adults who have been
unable to provide an environment within which the child can
grow, develop, and learn. This failure is profound, as it highlights

the complexities of raising children and the range of skills, supports, and resources that are required to do it successfully. Any parent, when being honest about their experience of parenthood, will acknowledge the times when they have felt so close to doing things that would have hurt, injured, or scarred their children. Thankfully, the very vast majority of adults are able, when faced with these intensities of feelings, to contain them. This is facilitated not only by the emotional security of the parent, but also by the context within which the parent is living being conducive to promoting their own resilience to mental health difficulties.

The Office for National Statistics (2000) established that one child in five in the general population of the United Kingdom is likely to have a mental health problem—that is, to have experienced or to be experiencing difficulties in relationships and in learning that significantly interfere with personal development and require help in addition to that provided by family and friends. Research in Oxfordshire has shown that in residential units for children in care, as many as 96% of looked-after children have a psychiatric disorder (McCann, James, Wilson, & Dunn, 1996). This higher percentage of mental health problems is particularly significant when one explores further the outcomes for looked-after children.

- Of care-leavers, 75% have no educational qualification of any kind, compared to 6% of the general population (DoH, 1997).

- Children in care are ten times more likely to be excluded from school; only 12% of care-leavers go on to further education, compared with 68% of the general population; only one in 300 care-leavers go on to university, compared with two in five of the general population.

- With regard to employment, more than 50% of young people leaving care after the age of 16 are unemployed; 17% of young women leaving care are pregnant and already mothers.

- One quarter of care-leavers have a child by the age of 16; half are mothers within the 18–20 months after leaving care.

- Between one quarter and one third of young homeless people have been in care, young people with a care background being 60 times more likely to be homeless than others.

- Among prisoners, 30% of adults and 38% of young offenders have been in care.

The Government has responded to this catalogue of disaster by its White Paper, *Modernising Social Services* (DoH, 1998). This is an array of processes for transforming Social Services in order to improve the service that children receive and, in particular, improve the outcomes for children in care.

In a recent major summary of post-Children Act research, it was found that children were expressing clear worries about their health and the risks to their educational attainment and their futures as a result of being in care. The uncertainty concerning placement stability and the prospect of isolation upon leaving care caused particular anxiety (DoH, 2001). The failure of the care system to respond appropriately to the enormous needs of looked-after children is the second "family" of adults to fail to provide the appropriate environment within which children and adolescents can grow and develop into adulthood. By illustrating with three case studies, I hope to demonstrate that work with violent adolescents in the care system is a complex process, involving a wide range of professionals, carers, and family adults to join together to take collective responsibility to meet the needs of these difficult and disturbing young people.

Tasks of adolescence

As a developmental stage, adolescence is perhaps one of the most complex and stretching both for the adolescent and for those who surround them. Adolescents are coping with major physical changes triggered by reaching a critical weight. There is a massive growth spurt and the development of secondary characteristics that take place over a number of years. Physical and hormonal changes result in changes in the emotional state and heightened awareness of sexuality. For some this is an exciting time, but for others the confusion and dilemmas are overwhelming.

During adolescence, young people are expected to take greater responsibility for themselves, their possessions, and their work. There is also the process of separation and reestablishment of a new relationship with the family of origin. Critically, during this period young people develop their ideas about how to make decisions about the way they live, their priorities and beliefs, and about what is right and wrong. In doing this, they draw on and are powerfully influenced by the beliefs and behaviours of their families and community. In forming these ideas, young people necessarily go through periods of questioning the beliefs of their carers, trying out different ideas, and they often adopt values that are not acceptable to some adults. The development of a moral code is closely linked to the negotiation of peer relationships; finding like-minded friends, joining a group, and deciding how and where to fit in is a major challenge for all young people—particularly so for those with low self-esteem, poor social skills, and communication difficulties. The absence of a stable base within the home environment frustrates the capacity of adolescents to engage successfully in the process of growing up, leaving behind childhood dependency and seeking out new people outside the family to enjoy friendship and intimacy (Talbot, 2002).

Containment: "Peter"

Peter was a 14-year-old adolescent with a diagnosis of attention deficit disorder. He had experienced severe family breakdown and had been in care for the past three years. He was referred to an adolescent unit after punching his consultant psychiatrist in the face. He had a history of violent behaviour and had made unsubstantiated allegations of sexual abuse by care staff.

Peter's mother had died in childbirth. His father had married his nanny and had had another child. His father then left his stepmother, who later placed the boy in social-service care. He had had sporadic contact with both his stepmother and his father. He had a violent and antagonistic relationship with his brother from his father's second marriage and was extremely angry about his father's remarriage.

Four months after his admission to the adolescent unit, I became Peter's individual psychotherapist, his previous psychotherapist having left the unit. Peter was enraged, and while not refusing to see me, he made direct reference to how he was going to make my life a misery. He would attend the sessions and spend up to 40 minutes telling me how disgusting I was and how useless psychotherapy was, regaling me with stories about how he had hurt and terrified the psychotherapist he had seen a few years previously. What began as verbal abuse turned physical: he began first to kick and then attempt to punch. He could spend approximately 10 minutes in a session reflecting on his experiences of the week, but in so doing he would soon lose control and would need to be removed from therapy by members of the nursing team. On leaving therapy, he would calm down quickly and become both remorseful and embarrassed. At times, I felt enormously punitive towards Peter. He seemed so desperate for me to hurt him and reject him, and I felt close to acting that out, squeezing that arm just a bit tighter than strictly necessary. These feelings became more pronounced when Peter spent a few sessions with legs around his neck, trousers pulled down, anus visible, inviting me to bugger him. He was trying to confirm his view of adults as abusive and punitive through projecting his aggressive feelings. Working with him required a team, capable collectively of containing both his and their own anxiety.

Containing these anxieties is easier said than done. The pressure for effective containment of looked-after children is greater because of the initial failure of the container within which young people were to grow and develop. Peter's experience of twelve changes in residential placement over three years had been a further demonstration to him of the lack of capacity of adults to contain him successfully. Effective containment is a skill that can be developed in adults when they pay attention to the following factors (Irvine, 2000).

    To be a successful container, it is first and foremost important to be consistent. This is not the same as being rigid. Consistency is about being flexible within defined boundaries. Adults need to know where the boundaries are and be confident, so that they can convey these boundaries to young people. Adults also need to be observers, taking note of the behaviour and feelings expressed by the child and themselves, using their understanding of their own feelings to know what the young person could be communicating by his or her behaviour. Adults also need to be able to negotiate. This does not mean imposing their own views, but being able to look at all the possibilities and work towards an agreed approach with the young person. These negotiations take place within the consistent boundaries that they have established, providing an important model from which young people can learn. It is also important that adults are able to remember what the primary task is at every moment in their interactions with the young person. Essentially this means being focused on what is important in the moment and not being distracted into activities that detract from the capacity of the adult to face the adolescent as another human being.

This process requires adults to create a space for thinking between feeling and acting. In many situations, young people are moving very quickly from feeling to acting without thinking about what is happening. Adults can often also do this, but the capacity to pause and think about what to do next in psychological terms is the process of metabolizing the projections, processing them, and being able to return them through interaction with the child in a way that enables growth, development, and safety for the adolescent. Enabling this means being able to be reasonable and follow through with young people, clear that one remains connected to the child no matter what the choices they make in a particular situation, and being available to enable the child to use the resource of the adult to learn from past experience and develop greater options in future situations. Self-awareness in the adult is critical to their capacity to remain thoughtful in response to the young person. This requires adults to be clear about how they are feeling, how this is affecting them, and their capacity to respond appropriately to the young person. Adults who feel caught up with their own problems will not find it easy to be available to the young person. Unless adults are conscious of what is happening to them, they might not be able to stop their anxieties affecting their interactions with adolescents.

This is particularly important when being aware of how power and authority are being used. Being in a position of authority brings a responsibility to use it wisely and in the best interests of the adolescent. Authority exercised punitively further crushes and stifles the adolescent. Investing in difficult and disturbing children can be difficult, but a capacity to work on repairing relationships and be available to adolescents enables them to find new experiences. This involves patience, tolerating difference and confusion, and working from a position of striving to understand. It is only when the adolescent feels appropriately contained and invested-in that real work can begin.

Effective containment by adults of young people's anxiety requires that effective systems are in place for the containment of the anxiety of adults in direct contact with the child. Failures in our capacity to take collective responsibility for providing effective care for looked-after children—it is the lack of attention to this process that leads to breakdowns in partnerships between agencies and professionals, when the child ceases to be a human being and, rather, becomes a problem to be managed.

> Peter is now at college. He lives in a residential home and has weekly contact with both parents. He often overnights with his mother and brother. Peter returned to see me for seven months after his discharge, travelling two hours each way on public transport and only missing one session during flooding. In the final sessions, we began to talk about the loss of each other, and he reflected that Tuesdays would never be the same again. They aren't.

The long haul: "Gavin"

Gavin was an 11-year-old when I first met him. His mother had just died, and he and his father were left alone. At the time he was managing at school, and his father refused to engage with services. I met him again later, at age 13, when he was experiencing difficulty at school, truanting, and behaving destructively in the home. His father engaged with his son in family therapy and was seen by the family therapist in the child and adolescent mental health service. This work progressed over a year, and while there were some improvements, there had been

deterioration in Gavin's behaviour, and he was becoming engaged in a range of delinquent activity, drug-taking, and alcohol consumption.

For the first time he agreed to meet on an individual basis, and
I saw him three times. After the third session, he said that he
was interested in the conversations that we'd had, but that he
didn't want to attend on a regular basis. The substance of our
conversations had been the difficulties with his here-and-now
experiences, and this was the first time that he had had any
significant contact with me. Six months later, I was informed
that the local authority had accommodated him, and he was in
a local residential unit. I began attending his regular child-care
reviews, contributing to the discussion with the range of professionals involved and advising residential workers on management of his disruptive and often aggressive behaviour; I also
offered Gavin the opportunity of coming to see me. He rejected
these offers consistently for a year, but then he popped into the
child and adolescent clinic and asked if he could make an
appointment to see me. This began a six-month period of sporadic contact, cancelled appointments, and the occasional session, focusing largely on his relationships with the range of
carers and his consistent refusal to participate in educational
activities.

He talked of his occasional violent outbursts, largely directed
against property but often injuring other young people and
adults by accident, justifiable responses to the frustrations he
was feeling. Slowly he settled into a regular appointment. He
then began to make links between his current experiences and
his past experiences, demonstrating a high level of insight and
an increased capacity to tolerate the range of emotions he experienced both within and outside the sessions.

Work with Gavin was at times intensely frustrating, and the
temptation within the system to blame him and each other for
the failure to actively engage him in therapeutic help and education was difficult to manage. This process involved the development of an effective partnership between the residential unit,

his social worker, and myself as Gavin's potential child and adolescent mental health worker. Also, it required an effective partnership with his father, who—while adamant that he would not receive him at home—was still a key factor in his life. The capacity (described in a previous section of this chapter) to work at containing the anxiety of the young person and the adults became more crucial in the context of inter-agency working. Through utilizing the childcare review, engagement with the broad partnership of housing, education, education welfare, and so on, was also possible. The role that I took up was of promoting the capacity of the system to remain focused on its primary purpose: that of providing a containing environment within which Gavin could manage the difficulties currently experienced and make choices for his future.

The challenge to professionals involved was to pay attention to meeting Gavin's day-to-day needs. At the same time, we needed to remain able to reflect on the forward planning that needed to take place and engage with him in decision making and planning in relation to his care. The residential staff had enormous difficulty in understanding Gavin's behaviour. It seemed to them that whenever progress was being made and staff thought that they were establishing a good relationship with him, he would destroy his bedroom or public areas of the residential unit. There were times when they were enormously frustrated that I was not able to magically produce answers to the difficulties and engage him in "treatment" that would sort out his behaviour.

The process of consultation was to enhance the capacity of residential staff to work at being containers, but also to build resilience within Gavin to manage his mental health difficulties. Underlying the negative behaviour was a clear depression. At times, staff became overwhelmed when he would refuse consistently to get out of bed, threaten to harm himself, and become enormously morbid, sarcastic, and abusive to staff and other young people. Staff felt helpless to control the periods of heavy drinking and drug use, which were flaunted in front of them, with Gavin articulating his rights under the UN Convention of the Child whenever they tried to take action to contain his behaviour. Encouraging a focus on building resilience enabled staff to begin to understand and boost positive aspects of his behaviour. For him, this focused on developing his relationship with his father and a maternal aunt with whom he'd earlier had a close relationship. The facilitation of his contact with both father and aunt was an important factor in attending to his day-to-day needs.

All adolescents have a basic need to be thought about and to be cared for. This is immensely difficult with high levels of turnover of staff and residential workers, but the importance of the stability of Gavin's social worker throughout this period cannot be underestimated. She provided the one consistent adult who remained capable of thinking about him and holding him in mind, withstanding enormous attacks and attempts to undermine and disempower her. She was able to develop the capacity of holding clear and firm boundaries with confidence and compassion and was active in supporting his education. The more consistently she was able to do this, the more he began to talk with her about some of his difficulties, often sharing his feelings of despondency and hopelessness.

Within the community, a sense of connectedness to a broader network was developed through Gavin's contact with the Young People in Care support group. This group had been drawn together by the Social Services Department to involve young people in policy-making with regard to the care system. Gavin became an active member of this group and demonstrated periods of exceptional leadership. This was boosted, and he was given increasing responsibility within the residential unit. Extending his talents and skills covered a broader range of activities. Along with other young people in the residential unit, he was offered the opportunity to participate in a range of leisure activities. He demonstrated ability as a swimmer and participated in a local swimming club. He experienced a constant tension between undertaking these activities and engaging in delinquent activity with a group of young people in the community. Also, he was dramatically affected by the turbulence of the residential unit, often experiencing the behaviour of other young people as intolerable.

In interactions with staff, Gavin's intelligence was often intimidating, but staff were able to engage him effectively in more and more productive ways, managing the times when he used his intelligence in a manipulative and destructive way. His positive social skills enabled him to establish connections with staff, who found him likeable a lot of the time. By supporting him in developing a capacity to plan and control his environment, they built more opportunities to reflect on his behaviour and experience. As he developed more and more trusting relationships, he shared more broadly his experiences and feelings and utilized different staff in various ways to make sense of what was happening to him and attempt to come to terms with it. It was during this period that he began to become interested in meeting for one-to-one sessions.

> Gavin was adamant in early sessions that he was not prepared to talk about the past. He reported being tired of being told to come and see the therapist to sort out his past, and instead talked about his day-to-day preoccupations, relationships with peers and care staff, his social worker, his father, and his frustrations and sporadic contact with his aunt. Soon, Gavin was raising the death of his mother, and he began making links between his current experience and the past. At this point, the possibility of working in a more structured way became possible. Gavin accepted the suggestion of a regular two sessions a week. The experience of working with him raised enormous challenges to the traditional understanding of the psychotherapeutic role. Gavin talked of the importance of the presence of the *possibility* of psychotherapy, as demonstrated through my participation in the strategy reviews. He acknowledged awareness of my involvement with the residential staff and his social worker and talked of deliberating missing sessions in the past to see whether I would refuse to see him.

> In the mid-point of therapy, Gavin became verbally abusive and threatened aggression. He spoke of fantasies of damaging me and asserted that I was trying to control his life and his thoughts. This precipitated a period of intense depression as he worked on the dual loss of his mother and his father at the time of his mother's death. He began to reflect on his father's loss and inability to engage with him emotionally, and he linked both his positive and negative experiences of his father to his

experience in therapy. As he was able increasingly to tolerate the pain that he experienced, he began to link his violent outbursts and desire to destroy his environment to intense feelings of isolation, panic and anxiety.

Gavin's engagement in the therapeutic relationship was possible only because of the increased containment he experienced in his relationships with adults in the residential setting and broader system. Resilience in the professional system was facilitated by attention to developing effective communication between all adults and between agencies in relation to care. The struggle to maintain a child-centred approach in discussions between agencies was challenged as the needs of particular agencies or organizations were emphasized. The resolutions of these tensions in the interests of childcare were often achieved, and for all involved the capacity of adults to hold the different aspects of Gavin, in an attempt at seeing him as a whole human being, dramatically facilitated both the work with him and the capacity of the adults to work together. For the professionals, often the hardest job was giving up the fantasy of a magical solution. Working through the disappointment that there was no other way but to persevere and remain responsive to his needs at times undermined the capacity of the adults to hold hope that their perseverance, thought and attention would make a significant difference to his experience of the world and his response to it.

Lost and found: "Jeremy"

Jeremy was 14 years old. He was referred as he was physically attacking his foster father. Yet another placement was about to break down, and he faced his fourth move in a year. Each placement had broken down as a result of violence. When he attended the first meeting, his foster mother and father and one of his foster parents' children, aged 17, accompanied him. The family described a situation where at school Jeremy was doing well, and at home he was a nightmare to live with. His refusal to participate in activities outside the home intensified relationships, and his foster brother talked of feeling like hurting him when he saw him attack his father. His foster father described apparently sudden and unexpected outbursts where Jeremy would kick, punch, scratch, and bite him—sometimes being consoled by being held, but at other times storming off to his bedroom and locking the door. His foster mother appeared helpless to know what could be done. With the family's agreement, a strategy meeting was called with the school and his social worker.

The history revealed that Jeremy had been taken into care after living an erratic lifestyle with his mother, a prostitute and known heroin addict. He had been shunted between his mother and his paternal grandparents, who were now too elderly to able to look after him. He had been in care for a year, and four foster placements had broken down—the first after two weeks, the second lasting nine weeks, and the subsequent placements for a number of months. At the strategy meeting it was revealed that throughout Jeremy's school life he had maintained good attendance and was progressing well in all areas. His social worker reported that prior to being taken into care, the one thing that had been maintained was his attendance at the same primary school, where he had developed strong friendships with a number of children, spending a lot of time with them and their families. She described the painful sight of him sitting on a step while his mother was working. The Head of Year identified that there was a particular teacher to whom Jeremy talked. He loved English and, given half the chance, he would spend hours talking to the English teacher about topics they were studying. He had never approached the Health drop-in centre where there was a school nurse and youth counsellor present. While the school was aware of the changes of address, they felt that they could not recognize the boy who was being described.

Jeremy was adamant that he did not want to come to therapy, that it was nobody's business but his own. The foster parents were prepared to continue with his placement and agreed to attend a parenting group for parents of adolescent children. His foster brother could recall times when he had enjoyed listening to music with Jeremy; a band that they both liked was playing in London, and his foster brother suggested that he take Jeremy to the concert. The school environment seemed to provide Jeremy with a sense of stability and was being used as a haven of sanity in the midst of a life that seemed dominated by an unfathomable noise in his head. Jeremy said that he wanted to see his mother, which was currently not allowed under the terms of the care order, and also said that he missed his friends from his primary school, with whom he no longer had any contact. His social worker undertook to explore contact with one of his friends, with whom he had often stayed over. Jeremy was due his annual health check, and it was agreed that this would take place in school with the school nurse. The Head of Year agreed that the English teacher would create more spaces to talk with Jeremy, as he was still adamant that this was the only person he was prepared to talk to.

When going for his medical, Jeremy saw a poster for an anger management group run by the adolescent counselling service. He asked the nurse about it, but did not discuss or reveal any information about his difficulties. Systemic difficulties prevented all the agreed action from occurring quickly, but within six months Jeremy was able to stay overnight with his friends, re-establishing contact with boys from other schools. In talking with his English teacher, he acknowledged feeling ashamed of his behaviour. He asked what the teacher thought about the anger management group, but he was unable to join it as it was already halfway through its cycle. The physical attacks on his foster father continued but became lower in intensity and less frequent. The foster parents reported having found the parenting classes useful in giving them a range of ways of understanding Jeremy's behaviour. They reflected on how useful this would have been when their own child was an adolescent, but they still felt that they needed more to understand his life.

Jeremy agreed to join the foster family for a series of six sessions. He was not interested in talking about his experience with his mother, only that he missed her and that he wanted to see his father. His father had left his mother because of her drug-taking when Jeremy was two, and he had had no contact with him since then. Jeremy attended the anger management class, which helped him significantly in beginning to predict when he felt that he was losing control and to develop strategies to diffuse this. He continued to see the adolescent counsellor for a 12-session block, asking at the end for referral to see a psychotherapist. Family therapy had been occurring on a monthly basis during this period. Sporadic contact was established with his mother, and attempts were being made to contact his father.

This story illustrates the critical importance to looked-after children of the maintenance of stability within education. Recent research has clearly demonstrated that where education placements remain stable, there is less breakdown in foster placements, and, as shown in this case, they can provide a haven and source of help leading on to more intensive work at a pace with which the young person is able to cope (DoH, 2001).

Conclusion

These three case studies illustrate a range of different responses to different children in different contexts exhibiting violent and aggressive behaviour linked to their experiences of being placed in care, and demonstrate the intensity of work that is required to create contexts in which the adolescent is able to engage with adults in the process of healing. In concluding, I think it is important that we re-visit the primary anxiety, referred to at the beginning of the chapter, which children being received into care evoke. The evidence of parents being unable to care effectively for their children raises in all parents who are concerned about their parenting a relief that there are parents clearly worse than themselves. The uncomfortable feeling that other parents, other adults, hurt their children soon dims, as the focus becomes the problem child.

Corporate parenting responsibility lies with the local authority, and this implies that the local authority demands for the children they look after the same standard as for every child. We must be able to believe that these children are our children, that we bear a collective responsibility for their care and show commitment to provide the support, love, and attention that they require, that our fellow human beings have not been able to provide. Looked-after children need to be able to relate to the corporate parent as a real human being.

The care system can only succeed in meeting the needs of looked-after children if that care is totally child-centred, and the adults working collectively to meet those needs are able to retain a picture of the whole child rather than just the part for which they are responsible. Increasingly, local authorities are supporting the development of looked-after children participating in advocacy for other young people, and in developing and consulting on services, we have the beginnings of young people and adults accepting mutual responsibility for a collective future.

CHAPTER FIVE

Working with adolescents who want to kill themselves

Emily Cooney & Lynn Greenwood

E xam stress, bullying, abuse ... it is not unusual to read newspaper reports of adolescents whose experiences have driven them to suicide. While the "successful" cases may hit the headlines, less often reported are those young people whose attempts to overdose, cut their wrists, hang themselves, or end their lives in other ways have "failed".

What provokes such a severe crisis in an adolescent? While there is no quick and easy answer to such a question, perhaps it is about facing intolerable experiences at a time when the world feels an uncertain place. After all, adolescents find themselves negotiating dramatic physiological and emotional changes at the same time as they are being encouraged to re-negotiate the oedipal experience and step further outside the (sometimes questionable) security of the family and into a broader social environment. Where that environment feels threatening and where the home may be—at best—unsupportive and—at worst—neglectful or abusive, this transition can feel painfully impossible to achieve.

There are many parallels between adolescence and toddlerhood. In the case of the latter, Winnicott (1954, p. 263) stressed the importance of the mother's holding function as an essential part of an infant's emotional development, allowing him to "work through the consequences of instinctual experiences. . . . The mother's technique enables the infant's co-existing love and hate to become sorted out and interrelated and gradually brought under control from within in a way that is healthy." This capacity to contain is also crucial in adolescence, where the young person is attempting to separate from the family, establish a self-identity, and withstand physiological changes and charged sexual feelings.

A parent's capacity to tolerate an adolescent's rebellious behaviour, uncertainty, and rage is vital, enabling her* to learn that an emotion that may sometimes feel overpowering is not lethal. Sometimes, however, parents or caretakers are not able to contain these emotions—and may even project their own intolerable feelings and experiences into the young person, exacerbating a sense of anxiety, powerlessness, and pessimism. Suicide can seem to be the only way to end the chaos and hopelessness. Yet the temptation to commit such an act begs the question that rage towards another or others has merely been directed towards the self.

Risk factors

When a young person comes into treatment, gauging the risk of suicide is an important part of the assessment process. Much of the research into risk factors is oriented towards the general population rather than adolescents as a sub-group. That said, the findings highlight considerations for the assessment of suicide potential and provide a context for the specific predictive factors in this age group. However, such research has its limitations. First, correlations do not provide information regarding causality but indicate only that the phenomena are somehow related. Thus, a risk factor may be a precursor, a consequence, a precipitating factor, or a corollary to suicidal expression. Second, the base rate of suicide is relatively low, so the data cannot be used predictively. Small and potentially random fluctuations in rate can skew data significantly in ways that may not reflect clinically meaningful relationships.

---

*In this chapter, for ease of expression, the feminine pronoun has been used for all otherwise unspecified adolescents.

Furthermore, many of the risk factors are so broad that they could relate to large sections of the general population and are therefore not useful for prediction.

The SAD PERSONS mnemonic (Hudson & Ward, 1997; Patterson, Dohn, Bird, & Patterson, 1983) provides a useful reminder of issues to consider when reviewing risk indicators for an individual.

Sex: Females are more likely to attempt suicide; males are more likely to "complete" it (Beautrais, 2000; Pirkis, Burgess, & Jolley, 2002; Pritchard, 1992); the estimated ratio of female to male attempted suicides is two/three to one, with males aged between 15 and 24 three to five times more likely to succeed.

Age: Recently, in Australasia, the rate has increased for males between the ages of 15 and 24; suicides appear to peak between the ages of 30 and 34 and for males over 80 (Hudson & Ward, 1997).

Depression: Affective disorders are associated with a higher risk of suicide and attempted suicide, both in the general population and in young people; case-control studies estimate that young people suffering from mood disorders are up to 27 times more likely to die by suicide than those not suffering from such a disorder (Beautrais, 2000).

Previous history of attempts: This is the strongest predictor in several studies, with multiple attempts raising the risk of "completing" suicide (Beautrais, 2000; Brent, 1997; Larzelere, Smith, Batenhorst, & Kelly, 1996; Renaud, Brent, Birmaher, Chiapetta, & Bridge, 1999).

Ethanol/drug abuse: In both the general population and young people, abuse and other substances is a significant risk factor (Beautrais, 2000; Brent, 1997). This is particularly true when combined with a mental disorder, possibly owing to increased impulsivity and disinhibition associated with intoxication. The "lethal triad" of antisocial behaviour, depression, and substance abuse is associated with an elevated risk of suicide in young people, especially males (Greenhill & Waslick, 1997; Larzelere et al., 1997).

Rational thinking deficit: Reduced problem-solving ability and thought disorder associated with psychosis have also been linked with an elevated risk of suicide in the general population (Hudson & Ward, 1997). While only a small proportion of adolescents who die by suicide suffer from psychotic disorders, the risks associated with psychosis are high (Beautrais, 2000; Brent, 1997).

Sickness: Unsurprisingly, given risk factors discussed above, chronic physical or emotional illness is associated with increased risk.

Organized plan: The presence, detail and lethality of a plan is a primary risk indicator (Hudson & Ward, 1997). The availability of the means to commit suicide is also associated with higher risk (Beautrais, 2000; Brent, 1997).

No spouse: The absence of a life partner is a risk factor in the general population (Hudson & Ward, 1997). Interpersonal loss, such as the break-up of a romantic relationship, has been identified as a particular risk for adolescents, with boys at higher risk than girls (Greenhill & Waslick, 1997).

Support lacking: The absence of support combined with stressful life events increases the risk of suicide in adolescents. Factors associated with increased risk include adverse family circumstances (such as parental separation, parental psychopathology, and conflict between parents and children), conflict with authority (e.g. suspension from school or legal proceedings), and sexual abuse (where severity seems to raise the risk of suicide attempts substantially (Fergusson, Horwood, & Lynskey, 1996). A history of suicide in the family is a particular risk for the general population, independent of a history of mental illness (Qin, Agerbo, & Mortensen, 2002). Furthermore, "contagion" suicide is a phenomenon to which young people appear to be particularly vulnerable (Beautrais, 2000).

In addition, after some contention, research has emerged that suggests that gay, lesbian, and bisexual young people are at increased risk for a range of mental health problems, particularly multiple psychiatric disorders, suicidal ideation, and suicide attempts (Beautrais, 2000). Beautrais speculates that the absence of a correlation between suicide completion and sexual orientation may be associated with difficulties in establishing sexual orientation after someone has taken her own life.

The referral

Gathering information directly from the young person is an important component of risk assessment and on-going support and assistance. However, she will rarely be the sole source of information—and may even be "beyond" seeking help. The initial referral may come from friends, teachers, family members, and professionals who have become concerned about he adolescent's mood and behaviour.

> In the case of "Jamie", a 16-year-old, three of his friends alerted the school counsellor that they were worried about his behaviour on the previous Saturday, when he had become extremely drunk and used substantial quantities of cannabis and speed. The counsellor spent some time with Jamie's friends, encouraging them to talk and listening carefully to all they had to say. The counsellor also made enquiries and found that he had a good relationship with his form teacher. She enlisted this man's help in encouraging Jamie to talk to her and asked him to be part of the team that would support the boy through his crisis.

It is important to take every referral seriously—particularly when it comes from peers, who may fail to act again if their request for help is minimized or ignored.

This type of report is generally the first opportunity to assess risk and may also help to identify the adults who should form part of a team that will support the adolescent through the crisis. The team needs to be mobilized rapidly in order to provide containment and consider on-going options.

The interview

Regardless of the context of the interview, it is crucial to establish a climate of empathy and emotional robustness. The professional demonstrates a commitment to understanding the extent and intensity of an adolescent's pain by creating the time and emotional space to explore it fully. For a young person such as Jamie, ensuring that the meeting is uninterrupted shows that his needs are important and—during his time—will not be subsumed by other demands. An honest approach to the individual's right to confidentiality (and the limits of that) creates a context of open collaboration, balanced by a commitment to the young person's safety—even when she is unable to take responsibility for this herself.

Many adolescents find verbal communication difficult and lack the social and emotional sophistication to respond fully in words. For this reason, the professional's approach should be flexible and creative. The practitioner may begin by trying to encourage the client to talk with general comments and observations or open questions. Where responses are minimal (perhaps no more than a shrug), one can move on gently to closed questions that ask for specific facts. Another approach is to interpret the adolescent's emotional state ("I have a sense that you're feeling really desperate at the moment") and ask her to confirm or reject these interpretations. An erroneous interpretation can spur a disengaged young person into more active communication.

Paper, pencils, and crayons provide a non-verbal form of communication that permits doodling, drawing, or writing and minimizes the discomfort of long silences, eye contact, and emotionally intense material—another way of "speaking" what may be felt to be unspeakable. "Jane", 15 years old, acknowledged that she had feelings of despair but was unable to verbalize these. With crayons and paper, she drew pictures of bloody knives and nooses and wrote down words that illustrated her violent despair. This provided the practitioner with a "way in" to Jane's sense of rage and hopelessness.

The clinician can also use pen and paper to write down information and enhance the sense of open, collaborative exploration as opposed to a formal interview. Graphic representations (such as pie charts or "will to live" thermometers) help to define the intensity of suicidal thoughts in different situations—and thus elicit important information about high-risk situations and the degree of ambivalence. Emphasizing the variation in the intensity of the desire to die highlights to the adolescent that suicide is irreversible while emotions—even though extremely distressing at times—are transient.

The speed with which the clinician moves from general to more specific exploration of the young person's wish to die will depend on the strength and length of their relationship and the context of the interview. If the client knows that the purpose of the session is to explore suicidality, she will anticipate direct and specific interventions. This may also be true where the session is part of ongoing therapy, where an alliance exists and the clinician is aware of risk indicators and has already stated and/or acted on his responsibility for the young person's safety.

Moving gradually but firmly towards a more direct exploration allows both clinician and client to become accustomed to the anxiety of discussing suicidal thoughts. It also communicates that the discussion is vital. Furthermore, a tentative approach to critical issues is less often met with false denial or resistance (Hudson & Ward, 1997) than is immediate, closed questioning. Professionals are often reluctant to ask directly about suicidal impulses and may attribute this to a fear that such questions could strengthen them. Anxiety about "naming the beast" may relate to concerns about the responsibility associated with knowledge as much as concerns about increasing the risk by talking about it.

The therapist's use of language—and choice of words—can help or hinder. For example, "externalizing" the suicidal impulses (White & Epston, 1990) supports the client in perceiving herself to be separate from the problem. There is a subtle but important distinction between talking about "suicidal urges" rather than "being suicidal". "Locating" a problem "inside" someone could mean that attempts to resolve the situation are destructive rather than nurturing. Language can encourage a young person to join the professional and other members of the team in a battle against the wish to die, or it can make them a passive recipient of treatment for a person with mental health problems.

Typically, suicidality in adolescents coincides with stressful life events, such as difficult relationships; a sense of alienation, hopelessness and distrust, and conflicts with the law or the education system (cf. Beautrais, 2000; Shea, 1988). Asking about or reflecting on such events can be a fruitful "way in", allowing the professional to explore gently whether the young person feels so overwhelmed that she might have thoughts of taking her life and—perhaps more importantly—has a "plan" of how to do it. As research has demonstrated, the existence of such a plan is a critical risk indicator, particularly where there is a history of previous attempts. It is important, therefore, to determine whether the young person has access to the means to implement such a plan.

Someone who has a coherent, organized strategy to kill herself if—say—she fails exams in four months' time is arguably safer (at least, for the present) than is someone who experiences a sporadic, intense impulse to die and then goes on a drinking binge or takes drugs (particularly if abusing substances regularly).

The "supportive team"

The level of risk affects how that risk is contained—and *by whom*: what may be helpful in the short term can be counter-therapeutic in the longer term. A number of key issues affect such decisions.

The first is *who* should be responsible for working alongside the young person. This depends on factors such as whether the individual aware of the risk has the ability and mandate to contain it, whether additional support is required, and who should provide it.

When considering the question of responsibility, it is crucial to think about the strength of the adolescent's wish to die, coupled with access to the means to do so. Thinking about background and environment is, therefore, as important as considering her "internal landscape". High suicidality in an inpatient setting is arguably less risky than that in an outpatient context. Therefore, identification of resources and agencies can be critical. Services that help to contain the risk of suicide include primary and secondary care, acute psychiatric units, and secure facilities. Reviewing these options helps the professional or the team to identify the optimal setting.

Irrespective of setting, the clinician can do much to demonstrate her commitment to life-enhancing rather than life-destroying solutions to the young person's immediate dilemmas—and these courses of action are generally available whether or not the client endorses them. These include:

1. *Communication with members of the supportive/professional network*

This network can include parents, foster carers, teachers, the GP, members of secondary mental health services, inpatient services, and/or the local emergency service. Such communication may involve generating a referral for assessment or treatment and talking to agencies individually or together. Involving the young person as much as possible—for instance, encouraging her to attend meetings at which her care is discussed, ensuring she receives copies of correspondence, engaging her in the process of writing letters and drafting minutes—encourages her to take active responsibility (as far as possible and realistic) for her own treatment.

2. *Developing a risk-containment plan*

The language of the risk-containment plan should be understood easily by the young person and reflect the way she communicates. (A graphic form of the plan can help to ensure its clarity.) This helps to ensure her involvement and models to everyone the importance of working *with* rather than *on* the client.

Typically, such plans identify danger times and triggers, indicators of increased risk, and response strategies (i.e., what the adolescent can do to enable her to tolerate and manage emotional pain and what others can do to support her). They will also include contact details, identify who is responsible for various responses and areas of care, and document contingencies for an after-hours escalation of concern.

The planning process should also consider longer-term issues as the adolescent gradually internalizes the ability to fend off suicidal urges by finding alternative methods of dealing with problems that appear overwhelming. Any self-nurturing strategies that she may be able to use to moderate extreme distress should also be documented. These might include contacting someone for support; drawing or painting on her body rather than cutting; using distress-management techniques (such as relaxation exercises or distracting activities); writing and reading reminders or statements that she feels affirm her will to live rather than her wish to die.

3. *Increasing therapeutic contact*

It is important to consider that actions that serve to reduce anxiety in the short term can sometimes maintain suicidal behaviour (cf.

Linehan, 1993; Linehan & Kehrer, 1993, p. 424). Long-term therapy is not always readily available, and it is therefore important to consider how such a resource is used. The purpose of therapy must be clear to the team, which should be mindful of support that can be interpreted as contingent on suicidal behaviour. Where contact is increased, it should be oriented clearly towards monitoring and modifying suicidal urges. Similarly, it is important to take care where therapy is decreased or ended so that an important source of containment and support is not perceived to be "killed off".

4.   Increased supervision

Increased supervision can be implemented either in the community or in an inpatient or other residential setting. Where a hospital admission is not indicated, it may be important for members of an emergency or mobile nursing team to provide one-to-one supervision for a limited period at danger times. Such an initiative has considerable advantages, even though it is not typically part of a mental health service's "brief". It can help to ease a transition from inpatient to outpatient care and also involves the family in taking an active role in managing the risk from an early stage of recovery.

Where there is a diagnosis of psychotic features or a major depression with atypical features, an admission is generally wise. This is also true in cases where there are concerns about the young person's living situation.

5.   Support for carers

This is important—particularly where the young person is remaining in the community during treatment. Again, the supportive team should identify who can provide such support.

The impact on practitioners

While the primary focus is on keeping the young person safe, dealing with a suicidal adolescent can take its toll on the individual members of the professional team. Where the risk of suicide emerges within the context of longer-term therapy, it is helpful for the therapist to reflect on the nature of his role. Such a risk typically invites her to assume a more intrusive and active role: he is fighting for the part of the client that wants to live. Considering the impact of this helps to contain some of the potential for enactment of the emotions associated with the young person's wish to die.

Gorkin (1987) identifies five major themes in countertransference evoked in working with suicidal clients.

1.   *Withdrawal and disconnection*

Countertransference of this type is most likely where the patient is disengaged from life and presents as distant and unreachable. The practitioner's sense of profound detachment could reflect that of his client and preclude a meaningful encounter that would serve to raise awareness of immediate and increased risk.

2.   *Aggression*

Aggression in the countertransference can indicate that the client's suicidal behaviour reflects the wish of others that she did not exist. This could result in her behaving in a way that provokes aggression and serves to reinforce that belief. The foster-mother of thirteen-year-old "George" confided that she wanted to further her education but felt that George stood in her way of fulfilling that ambition. She admitted that she often reacted to him with exhaustion and anger—wishing that he were no longer an obstacle.

3.   *Omnipotent concern*

This can be experienced as a determination to "rescue" the patient single-handed. Gorkin (1987) suggests that this allows the therapist to avoid his own sense of anger and futility and also appears to fulfil the client's wish to be rescued and parented. Omnipotent concern is a common response in the face of the difficult family backgrounds often associated with adolescent suicidality. It is not unusual for a practitioner to harbour fantasies of "adopting" a young client and provide the love and support that she feels has been lacking.

4.   *Hopelessness and despair*

Hopelessness and despair are a common response to another person's wish to commit suicide, particularly where there is a continuing chronic difficulty with emotional regulation. Arguably, this is more unusual with adolescents, where the behaviour is more likely to be a relatively short-term problem.

4. *Jealousy*

A clinician's "jealousy" is thought to be associated with a patient romanticizing death—often seeing suicide as a way of "joining" a dead loved one. Here, the professional is "competing" with another preferred source of support. Such countertransference is not always clear: the practitioner may simply feel rejected and hurt that suicide continues to appear to be a desirable option.

> A mother had committed suicide when her son, "Andrew", was 12 years old. Andrew, now 17 years old, often referred to his mother, and her decision to take her own life, with a mixture of ambivalence and yearning. His therapist felt as though she were being pitted against an idealized, shadowy rival in a struggle that she was doomed to lose. Reflecting on her countertransference, she realized that she was angry with Andrew for "putting" her in an impossible position and with his mother for leaving *her* to "inherit" the adolescent's emotional distress.

> Andrew became enraged when his therapist was forced to cancel a session. Instead of feeling guilty and inadequate, the practitioner was able to reflect on the parallels between her sudden unavailability and that of Andrew's mother. The young man began to sob and then to speak, in gasps, about his fury. The session was a turning point in the therapeutic alliance and in the work itself.

Any member of the team (professionals, family, foster parents, and other carers) may experience any or all of these countertransference responses. Such responses can affect the way the team operates—and behaves towards members—and are, therefore, important to consider.

The therapist can draw on his countertransference to help her client make sense of the function of suicidal expression (attempts, verbalizations, self-destructive behaviour) and what *else* she may be trying to communicate ("I need containment." "I am furious because no one is there for me.").

Conclusion

When a young person expresses a wish to die, it is important to draw on all the resources available to support her. Therapy is one option—but it may not always be available, particularly in the longer term. Communication between team members is crucial so that the adolescent's suicidal impulses are both contained effectively and are not seen by her as overwhelming the very people who are there to help. It is also important to reflect on one's own emotional response—countertransference—to what can feel like a highly charged and delicate situation.

REFERENCES

Adler, A. (1908). Der Aggressionstrieb im Leben und in der Neurose. *Fortschritte der Medizin, 26*: 577–584.

Adler, A. (1958). *What Life Should Mean to You.* New York: Putnam Capricorn Books.

Aldice, O. (1975). *Play Fighting.* New York: Academic Press.

Arnold, L. (1995). *Women and Self-Injury: A Survey of 76 Women.* Bristol: Bristol Crisis Service for Women.

Balint, M. (1959). *Thrills and Regressions.* London: Hogarth Press.

Balint, M. (1968). *The Basic Fault: Therapeutic Aspects of Regression.* London: Tavistock Publications.

Beautrais, A. L. (2000). Risk factors for suicide and attempted suicide among young people. *Australian and New Zealand Journal of Psychiatry, 34*: 420–436.

Berdondini, L., Fantacci, F., & Genta, M. L. (submitted). Supervisione di insegnanti e interventi antibullismo nella scuola. *Psicologia dell'Educazione e della Formazione.*

Berdondini, L., & Genta, M. L. (2001). Perception of internal and external family boundaries by well-adjusted children, bullies and victims. In: T. M. Gehring, M. Debry, & P. K. Smith (Eds.), *The Family System Test (FAST): A New Approach to Investigate Family Relations in Clinical Research and Practice.* Hove: Psychology Press.

Berdondini, L., & Smith, P. K. (1996). Cohesion and power in the families of children involved in bully/victim problems at school: An Italian replication. *Journal of Family Therapy, 18* (1): 99–102.

Bion, W. R. (1967). *Second Thoughts.* New York: Jason Aronson.

Blos, P. (1962). *On Adolescence: A Psychoanalytic Interpretation.* New York: Free Press.

Boulton, M. J. (1994). The relationship between playful and aggressive fighting in children, adolescents and adults. In: J. Archer (Ed.), *Male Violence.* London: Routledge.

Bowers, L., Smith, P. K., & Binney, V. (1994). Perceived family relationships of bullies, victims and bully/victims in middle childhood. *Journal of Social and Personal Relationships, 11*: 215–232.

Brent, D. A. (1997). Practitioner review: The aftercare of adolescents with deliberate self-harm. *Journal of Clinical Psychology & Psychiatry, 38*: 277–286.

Bruch, H. (1973). *Eating Disorders: Obesity, Anorexia and the Person Within.* New York: Basic Books.

Brumberg, J. J. (1988). *Fasting Girls: The Emergence of Anorexia Nervosa as a Modern Disease,* Cambridge, MA: Harvard University Press.

Burgess, A. (1987). Abused to abuser. Antecedents of socially deviant behaviour. *American Journal of Psychiatry, 144*: 1431–1436.

Charles, A. V. (1986). Physically abused parents. *Journal of Family Violence, 1*: 343–355.

Chartier, J.-P., & Chartier, L. (1982). *Les Parents Martyrs.* Paris: Payot.

Cross, L. (1993). Body and Self in feminine development: Implications for eating disorders and delicate self-mutilation. *Bulletin of the Menninger Clinic, 57*: 41–68.

Cummings, E. M., Vogel, D., Cummings, J. S., & El Sheikh, M. (1988). Children's responses to different form of expression of anger towards adults. *Child Development, 60*: 1392–1404.

DoH (1997). *When Leaving Home Is Also Leaving Care.* Department of Health. London: HMSO.

DoH (1998). *Modernising Social Services.* Department of Health. London: HMSO.

DoH (2001). *The Children Act Now.* Department of Health. London: HMSO

du Bois, R. (1998). Battered parents: Psychiatric syndrome or social phenomenon. In: A. Z. Shwartzberg (Ed.), *The Adolescent in Turmoil.* Westport, CT: Praeger.

du Bois, R., Gaebele, S., & Schaal, C. (1987). "Der Beitrag von Kontaktstörungen zur Entstehung von intrafamilialer Gewalt—am Beispiel des Parent Battering." Paper given at the 25th Annual Conference of the Deutsche Gesellschaft für Kinder- und Jugendpsychiatrie, Dresden.

Dugas, M., Mouren, M., & Halfon, O. (1985). Le parents battus e leurs enfants. *Psychiatrie de l'enfant*, *28*: 185–219.

Eichelman, B. (1983). The limbic system and aggression in humans. *Neuroscience and Biobehavioral Revues*, *7*: 391–394.

Einarsen, S. (1999). The nature and causes of bullying at work. *International Journal of Manpower*, *20* (1/2): 16–27.

Erikson, E. H. (1950). *Childhood and Society*. New York: W. W. Norton.

Erikson, E. H. (1968). *Identity: Youth and Crisis*. New York: W. W. Norton.

Fairbairn, W. R. D. (1952). *Psychoanalytic Studies of the Personality*. New York/London: Routledge.

Farrell, E. (1995). *Lost for Words: The Psychoanalysis of Anorexia and Bulimia*. London: Process Press.

Favazza, A. (1987). *Bodies under Siege: Self Mutilation and Body Modification in Culture and Society*. Baltimore, MD: Johns Hopkins University Press.

Favazza, A. (1989). Why patients mutilate themselves. *Hospital and Community Psychiatry*, *40*: 137–145.

Favazza, A , & Contcrio, K. (1988). The plight of chronic self-mutilators. *Community Mental Health Journal*, *24* (1): 22–30.

Fergusson, D. M., Horwood, L. J., & Lynskcy, M. T. (1996). Childhood sexual abuse, and psychiatric disorder in young adulthood: II. Psychiatric outcomes of childhood sexual abuse. *Journal of the American Academy of Child & Adolescent Psychiatry*, *35*: 1365–1374.

Finnegan, R. A., Hodges, E. V. E., & Perry, D. G. (1998). Victimization by peers: Associations with children's reports of mother–child interaction. *Journal of Personality and Social Psychology, 75* (4): 1076–1086.

Freud, A. (1936). *The Ego and the Mechanisms of Defence. The Writings of Anna Freud, Vol. 2*. New York: International Universities Press, 1966.

Freud, S. (1920g). *Beyond the Pleasure Principle. S.E., 18*. London: Hogarth Press.

Freud, S. (1924d). The dissolution of the Oedipus Complex. *S.E., 19*.

Freud, S. (1930a). *Civilization and Its Discontents. S.E., 21*.

Gardner, A. R., & Gardner, A. J. (1975). Self-mutilation, obsessionality and narcissism. *British Journal of Psychiatry, 127*: 127–132.

Gehring, T. M., Debry, M., & Smith, P. K. (Eds.) (2001). *The Family System Test (FAST): A New Approach to Investigate Family Relations in Clinical Research and Practice.* Hove: Psychology Press.

Gehring, T. M., & Wyler, I. L. (1986). Family System Test (FAST): A three-dimensional approach to investigate human relationships. *Child Psychiatry and Human Development, 16*: 235–248.

Genta, M. L. (Ed.) (2002). *Il bullismo.* Rome: Carocci Editore.

Gilligan, C. (1982). *In a Different Voice: Psychological Theory and Women's Development.* Cambridge, MA: Harvard University Press.

Gilligan, J. (1996). *Violence.* London: Jessica Kingsley.

Gorkin, M. (1987). *The Uses of Countertransference.* Northvale, NJ: Jason Aronson.

Greenhill, L. L., & Waslick, B. (1997). Management of suicidal behaviour in children and adolescents. *The Psychiatric Clinics of North America, 20*: 641–666.

Harbin, H., & Madden, D. (1979). Battered parents: A new syndrome. *American Journal of Psychiatry, 136*: 1288–1291.

Hudson, S. M., & Ward, T. (1997). The assessment of suicide risk. In: H. Love & W. Whittaker (Eds.), *Practice Issues for Clinical and Applied Psychologists in New Zealand* (pp. 175–184). Wellington: New Zealand Psychological Society.

Humphrey, L. L. (1991). Object relations and the family system: An integrative approach to understanding and treating eating disorders. In C. Johnson (Ed.), *Psychodynamic Treatment of Anorexia Nervosa and Bulimia*, New York: Guilford Press.

Irvine, G. B. (2000). *Being a Container.* YoungMinds Training Materials, London.

Jacobs, B. W., & Isaacs, S. (1986). Pre-pubertal anorexia nervosa. *Journal of Child Psychology and Psychiatry.* (27): 237–250.

Jakob, A. (1994). *Battered Parents. Ergebnisse einer Umfrage.* Medical Dissertation, Tübingen University.

Kafka, J. (1969). The body as transitional object: A psychoanalytic study of a self-mutilating patient. *British Journal of Addiction, 81*: 641–649.

Lacey, J. H., & Evans, C. D. H. (1986). The impulsivist: A multi-impulsive personality disorder. *British Journal of Addiction, 81*: 641–649.

Ladame, F., & Perret-Catipovic, M. (1998). *Adolescence and Psychoanalysis.* London: Karnac.

Larzelere, R. E., Smith, G. L., Batenhorst, L. M., & Kelly, D. B. (1996). Predictive validity of the suicide probability scale among adolescents in group home treatment. *Journal of the American Academy of Child & Adolescent Psychiatry, 35*: 166–172.

Levens, M. (1995). *Eating Disorders and Magical Control of the Body: Treatment through Art Therapy.* New York/London: Routledge.

Liefooghe, A. P. D. (2001). *Voice, Discourse, Power: Accounts of Bullying at Work.* Unpublished PhD Thesis.

Liefooghe, A. P. D., & Mackenzie Davey, K. (2001). Bullying at work: The role of the organization. *European Journal of Work and Organizational Psychology, 10* (4): 375–392.

Likierman, M., & Urban, E. (1999). The roots of child and adolescent psychotherapy in psychoanalysis. In: M. Lanyado & A. Horne (Eds.), *Child and Adolescent Psychotherapy: Psychoanalytic Approaches.* New York/London: Routledge.

Linehan, M. M. (1993). *Cognitive Behavioural Treatment of Borderline Personality Disorder.* New York: Guilford Press.

Linehan, M. M., & Kehrer, C. A. (1993). Borderline personality disorder. In: D. H. Barlow (Ed.), *Clinical Handbook of Psychological Disorders* (pp. 396–441). New York: Guilford Press.

Mark, V., & Irvine, F. (1970). *Violence and the Brain.* New York: Harper & Row.

McCann, J. B., James, A., Wilson, S., & Dunn, G. (1996). Prevalence of psychiatric disorders in young people in the care system. *British Medical Journal, 313*: 1529–1530.

Miller, D. (1994). *Women Who Hurt Themselves: A Book of Hope and Understanding.* New York: Basic Books.

Office of National Statistics (2000). *Mental Health of Children and Adolescents in Great Britain: A Survey Carried out in 1999 by the Social Survey Division of the ONS on Behalf of the Department of Health, the Scottish Health Executive, and the National Assembly for Wales.* London: HMSO.

Olweus, D. (1977). Aggression and peer acceptance in adolescent boys: Two short-term longitudinal studies of ratings. *Child Development, 48*: 1301–1313.

Pao, P. N. (1969). The syndrome of delicate self-cutting. *British Journal of Medical Psychology, 42*: 195–206.

Patterson, W. M., Dohn, H. H., Bird, J., & Patterson, G. A. (1983). Evaluation of suicidal patients: The SAD PERSONS Scale. *Psychosomatics, 24*: 343–349.

Pattison, E. M., & Kahan, J. (1983). The deliberate self-harm syndrome. *American Journal of Psychiatry, 140* (7): 867–872.

Paulton, M. F., & Coombes, R. H. (1990). Youths who physically assault their parents. *Journal of Family Violence, 5*: 121–123.

Pepler, D. J., & Craig, W. M. (1995), A peek behind the fence: Naturalistic observations of aggressive children with remote audiovisual recording. *Developmental Psychology, 31*: 548–553.

Pirkis, J., Burgess, P., & Jolley, D. (2002). Suicide among psychiatric patients: A case-control study. *Australian and New Zealand Journal of Psychiatry, 36*: 86–91.

Pritchard, C. (1992). Youth suicide and gender in Australia and New Zealand compared with countries of the Western world, 1973–1987. *Australian and New Zealand Journal of Psychiatry, 26*: 609–617.

Qin, P., Agerbo, E., & Mortensen, P. B. (2002). Suicide risk in relation to family history of completed suicide and psychiatric disorders: A nested case-control study based on longitudinal registers. *Lancet, 360*: 1126–1130.

Randall, P. (1996). *Adult Bullying: Perpetrators and Victims.* London: Taylor & Francis.

Renaud, J., Brent, D. A., Birmaher, B., Chiapetta, L., & Bridge, J. (1999). Suicide in adolescents with disruptive disorders. *Journal of the American Academy of Child & Adolescent Psychiatry, 38*: 846–851.

Rigby, K. (1993). School children's perceptions of their families and parents as a function of peer-relations. *Journal of Genetic Psychology, 154*: 501–513.

Salmivalli, C., Lagerspetz, K. M. J., Bjorkqvist, K., Osterman, K., & Kaukiainen, A. (1996). Bullying as a group process: Participant roles and their relations to social status within the group. *Aggressive Behaviour, 22*: 1–15.

Schwartz, D., Dodge, K. A., Pettit, G. S., & Bates, J. E. (1997). The early socialization of aggressive victims of bullying. *Child Development, 68*: 665–675.

Shea, S. C. (1988). *Psychiatric Interviewing: The Art of Understanding.* Philadelphia, PA: W. B. Saunders.

Smith, P. K., & Myron-Wilson, R. (1998). Parenting and school bullying. *Clinical Child Psychology and Psychiatry, 3*: 405–417.

Steinmetz, S. K. (1978). Battered parents. *Society, 15*: 54–55.

Stern, S. (1991). Managing opposing currents: An interpersonal psychoanalytic technique for the treatment of eating disorders. In C. Johnson (Ed.), *Psychodynamic Treatment of Anorexia Nervosa and Bulimia*. New York: Guilford Press.

Sutton, J., & Smith, P. K. (1999). Bullying as a group process: An adaptation of the participant role approach. *Aggressive Behavior, 25*: 97–111.

Talbot, R. (2002). *Young Minds: Looking after the Mental Health of Looked-after Children*. Brighton: Pavilion.

Tantam, D., & Whittaker, J. (1992). Personality disorder and self-wounding. *British Journal of Psychiatry, 161*: 451–464.

Terr, L. (1991). Childhood traumas. An outline and overview. *American Journal of Psychiatry, 148*: 10–20.

Thomas, A., & Chess, S. (1977). *Temperament and Development*. New York: Brunner/Mazel.

Twemlow, S. W. (1995a). The psychoanalytical foundations of a dialectical approach to the victim/victimizer relationship. *Journal of the American Academy of Psychoanalysis, 23* (4): 545–561.

Twemlow, S. W. (1995b). Traumatic object relations configurations seen in victim/victimizer relationships. *Journal of the American Academy of Psychoanalysis, 23* (4): 563–580.

Twemlow, S. W. (2000). The roots of violence: Converging psychoanalytic explanatory models for power struggles and violence in schools. *Psychoanalytic Quarterly, 69* (4): 741–785.

Twemlow, S. W., Sacco, F. C., & Williams, P. (1999). A clinical and interactionist perspective on the bully–victim–bystander relationship. *Bulletin of the Menninger Clinic, 60* (3): 296–313.

van der Kolk, B. A., Perry, J. C., & Herman, J. L. (1991). Childhood origins of self-destructive behaviour. *American Journal of Psychiatry, 148* (12): 1665–1670.

VCC (1998). *Sometimes You've Got to Shout to Be Heard: Stories about Young People in Care*. London: Voice for the Child in Care.

Walsh, B. W., & Rosen, P. M. (1988). *Self-Mutilation: Theory, Research and Treatment*. New York: Guilford Press.

Warren, F. (1997). "What Is Self-harm?" Paper given at the 50th Anniversary Henderson Hospital Conference, on Managing Self-Harm, at St George's Hospital, London, 7 March (conference proceedings booklet, pp. 3–19).

White, M., & Epston, D. (1990). *Narrative Means to Therapeutic Ends*. New York: W. W. Norton.

Winnicott, D. W. (1953). Transitional objects and transitional phenomena. In: *Collected Papers*. New York: Basic Books; London: Tavistock, 1958.

Winnicott, D. W. (1954). The depressive position in normal emotional development. In: *Through Paediatrics to Psycho-Analysis*. London: Karnac, 1975.

Winnicott, D. W. (1965). *The Maturational Processes and the Facilitating Environment*. London: Hogarth Press.

Winnicott, D. W. (1986). *Home Is Where We Start From*. London/New York: W. W. Norton.

INDEX

Adler, A., 22, 25, 37, 40
adolescent development,
    "normal", vs. self-
    destructive behaviour, 9–
    11
affective disorders, and suicide
    risk, 75
affect modulation, 42
Agerbo, E., 76
aggression:
    adolescent, 44–45
    causes of, 39–41
        biological, 39–40
        developmental factors, 40–41
    childhood, 40, 42–45
    in countertransference, and
        suicidality, 83
    as creative, natural force, 40
aggressive victim, 23
aggressor(s):
    identification with,
        unconscious, ix

non-victimized, 23
alcohol abuse/dependency, 3, 8,
    51
    clinical example: "Gavin", 64–
    65
    as indicator for suicide risk, 80
    and parent battering, 47
Aldice, O., 43
Anderson, R., xiii
"Andrew": clinical example
    (jealousy in
    countertransference and
    suicidality), 84
anger management, 70
anorexia, 8, 16
    clinical example: 16-year-old
        youth, 19
    history of, 6
anti-bullying project, 26–29
anti-social tendencies, and parent
    battering, 47
Arnold, L., 9

attachment(s):
    deficiency and parent battering,
        50
    primitive, 12
attention deficit disorder, 60
Australia, 22
authority, conflict with, and
        suicide risk, 76
autistic traits, 41
    and parent battering, 47

Baden-Württemberg, 46
Balint, M., 44, 49
Batenhorst, L. M., 75
Bates, J. E., 23
Beautrais, A. L., 75, 76, 79
Berdondini, L., xiii–xiv, xv, xviii,
        21–37
Bertin, C., x
Binney, V., 23
Bion, W. R., 22–23
Bird, J., 75
Birmaher, B., 75
Bjorkqvist, K., 25
Blos, P., 3, 7
Bologna, 26
    University of, 26, 32
Bonaparte, M., x
Boulton, M. J., 43
Bowers, L., 23
Brent, D. A., 75, 76
Bridge, J., 75
British Postgraduate Medical
        Federation, University of
        London, xi
Bruch, H., 16
Brumberg, J. J., 7, 8
bulimia, 8, 16
    history of, 7
    and self-harm, 8
bullies, characteristics of, 21

bullying:
    clinical examples:
        "Marco", 31–33
        "Pierre", 33–35
        "Tamara", 30
    in communities, 21
    and family background, 22–24
    gender differences in, 23
    identification of, 35–36
    intervention programmes, 29–
        30
    and parental violence, 22
    role of bystanders in, 25–29
    school, systemic approach to,
        21–37
    self-reported, and family
        functioning, 23
    at work, 21
Burgess, A., 45
Burgess, P., 75
bystanders, role of in bullying,
        25–29

cannabis, 77
capital punishment, x
    see also death penalty
care, violence in, 57–72
    clinical examples:
        "Gavin", 63–68
        "Jeremy", 68–71
        "Peter", 60–63
Charles, A. V., 46
Chartier, J.-P., 46
Chartier, L., 46
Chess, S., 41
Chessman, C., x
Chiapetta, L., 75
child-battering, 39
    clinical examples:
        14-year-old youth: parent
            battering, 48

15-year-old girl: self-harm, 18–19

16-year-old youth: eating disorders, 19

17-year-old girl: parent battering, 54

20-year-old man: parent battering, 48

"Andrew": jealousy in countertransference and suicidality, 84

"Gavin": violence in care, 63–68

"George": suicidality, 83

"Jamie": violence in care, 77

"Jane": suicidality, 78

"Jeremy": violence in care, 68–71

"Marco": bullying, 31–33

"Peter": violence in care, 60–63

"Pierre": bullying, 33–35

"S.S.": parent battering, 53

"Tamara": bullying, 30–31

Columbine High School, Littleton, Colorado, 22

communication:
difficulties with, 60
non-verbal, and suicide risk, 78
symbiotic, 42
technology, 7

compulsive disorder, and parent battering, 47

contact disorders, and parent battering, 49–50

"contagion" suicide, 76

containment:
in care, clinical examples:
"Gavin", 63–68
"Peter", 60–63
developmental failures of, early, xviii

lack of, in childhood, 39
and suicide risk, 77

Conterio, K., 8–9

contraceptive pill, 2

Coombes, R. H., 46

Cooney, E., xiv, 73–85

countertransference and suicidality, 83

Cox, M., xi

crack cocaine, 2

Craig, W. M., 25

crime, petty, and parent battering, 47

Cross, L., 8

Cummings, E. M., 43

Cummings, J. S., 43

death penalty:
as group sadism, x
see also capital punishment

Debry, M., 24

deMause, L., ix

Department of Health, White Paper, 59

depersonalization and self-harm, 8

depression:
and parent battering, 47
sense of, violence as defence against, 3, 65
and suicide risk, 82

despair in countertransference, and suicidality, 83–84

development, sexual, 10–11

developmental disturbances, 12–15

dialectical social systems, 22

disconnection in countertransference, and suicidality, 83

Dodge, K. A., 23

Dohn, H. H., 75
drug abuse/dependency, 2–3, 5, 8,
    51
    and bullying, 35
        clinical example: "Pierre",
            34
    as indicator for suicide risk, 80
    mother's, clinical example:
        "Jeremy", 70
    and parent battering, 47
    and suicide risk, 75
        clinical example: "Jamie",
            77
    and violence in care, clinical
        example: "Gavin", 64–65
du Bois, R., xiv, xviii, 39–55
Dugas, M., 43
Dunn, G., 58

eating disorder(s), 3, 6–20
    clinical example: 16-year-old
        youth, 19
    and fear of loss and separation,
        16–17
    "multi-impulsivist", 8
    and parent battering, 47
    sub-clinical (SED), 8
    unit(s), 6
ecstasy, 2
Eichelman, B., 39
Einarsen, S., 21
El Sheikh, M., 43
emotional deprivation, 5
    and self-destructive
        behaviours, 15–17
"endless crisis state", 3
Epston, D., 79
Erikson, E. H., 1–2, 7
Europe, 22
Evans, C. D. H., 8
exclusionary processes, in social
    groups, 25

Fairbairn, W. R. D., 12–14
family background and bullying,
    22–24
family dynamics, 12
    and eating disorders, 16
family structure and parent
        battering, 50–52
Fantacci, F., 25, 26
fantasies, aggressive, 44–45
Farrell, E., 8, 16
father(s), absent, and bullying,
    24
Favazza, A., 7–9
Federn, E., x
Fergusson, D. M., 76
Ferrara, 32
"fight-or-flight" impulse, 40
Finnegan, R. A., 23
Freud, A., 45
Freud, S., x, xi, 40, 42, 45
    on aggression, 40
    Beyond the Pleasure Principle, 42
    Civilization and Its Discontents,
        40
    instinct theory of, 10–11
    Oedipus complex, "dissolution
        of the Oedipus Complex,
        The", 10–11
    secret committee, x

Gaebele, S., 46
Gardner, A. J., 9
Gardner, A. R., 9
"Gavin": clinical example,
        violence in care, 63–68
Gehring, T. M., 24
gender factors, and suicide risk,
    75
Genta, M. L., 21, 25–27
"George": clinical example,
        suicidality, 83
Gilligan, C., 7

Gilligan, J., 3
Glasser, M., xi
Glover, E., xi
Gorkin, M., 83
Graeco–Roman infanticide, ix
Greenhill, L. L., 75, 76
Greenwood, L., xiv, 1–4, 73–85
group sadism, x
group theory, Adler's, 25

Halfon, O., 43
Harbin, H., 45
helplessness, sense of, 3
Herman, J. L., 8–9, 15
heroin addiction, mother's, 69
Hitchum, 57
Hodges, E. V. E., 23
holding, maternal, importance of,
       73
hopelessness in
       countertransference and
       suicidality, 83–84
Horwood, L. J., 76
Hudson, S. M., 75, 76, 79
Humphrey, L. L., 16
hyperactivity, early, 42

identity:
   sense of, 51
       formation of, 1, 9, 74
   sexual, 10
illness, chronic physical or
       emotional, and suicide
       risk, 76
individuality, sense of, 9
infanticide, Graeco–Roman, ix
infantile distress, 41–43
infantile trauma, 39–55
instinct theory of psychological
       development, Freud's, 10
International Association for
       Forensic Psychotherapy, xi

Irvine, B., xv, 57–72
Irvine, F., 40
Isaacs, S., 8, 28
isolation, sense of, violence as
       defence against, 3
Italy, 24

Jacobs, B. W., 8
Jakob, A., 46
James, A., 58
"Jamie": clinical example,
       suicidality, 77
"Jane": clinical example,
       suicidality, 78
jealousy in countertransference
       and suicidality, 84
"Jeremy": clinical example,
       violence in care, 68–71
Jolley, D., 75

Kafka, J., 14
Kahan, J., 8
Kahr, B., ix–xii
Kaukiainen, A., 25
Kehrer, C. A., 82
Kelly, D. B., 75
Klein, M., x, xi, 22

Lacey, J. H., 8
Ladame, F., 2–3
Lagerspetz, K. M. J., 25
Larzelere, R. E., 75
Levens, M., 8
Liefooghe, A. P. D., xv, xviii, 21–
       37
Likierman, M., 11, 12
Linehan, M. M., 82
loss:
   fear of, 15
   interpersonal, and suicide risk,
       76
love, primary, 44

Lynskey, M. T., 76

Mackenzie Davey, K., 21
Madden, D., 45
magical thinking, 44
"Marco": clinical example,
    bullying, 31–33
marijuana, 2
Mark, V., 40
maternal reverie, 23
McCann, J. B., 58
mental illness and suicide risk, 76
Miller, D., 9
Moellenhoff, F., x
Mortensen, P. B., 76
Mouren, M., 43
"multi-impulsivist" eating
    disorders, 8
Myron-Wilson, R., 21, 22

narcissism, maternal, 16
narcissistic disturbances, 13–15
    and self-harm, 15
narcissistic wounding, 13, 20
neglect, 5
Norway, 21
Nunberg, H., x

object relations theory, 12
Oedipus complex, 10–11
Office for National Statistics, 58
Olweus, D., 21
omnipotence and powerlessness,
    and parent battering, 43,
    54
omnipotent concern in
    countertransference and
    suicidality, 83
omnipotent control, infantile
    sense of, 13
omnipotent fantasies, 43
Osterman, K., 25

over-identification, by parent with
    child, 5, 13

Pailthorpe, G., xi
Pao, P. N., 15
parasuicide, 8
parent:
    battering, 39–55
        clinical examples:
            14-year-old boy, 48
            17-year-old girl, 54
            20-year-old boy, 48
            "S.S.", 53–54
        dynamic considerations, 46–
            47
        therapeutic intervention, 52–
            55
    –child interactions, and parent
        battering, 48
parental psychopathology and
    suicide risk, 76
parental separation and suicide
    risk, 76
parenting, 71
    and bullying, 22
    corporate, local authority, 71
    dysfunctional, 22
    good-enough, 13–15
partner-battering, 39
Patterson, G. A., 75
Patterson, W. M., 75
Pattison, E. M., 8
Paulton, M. F., 46
peer victimization, 23
    see also bullying
penis envy, 11
Pepler, D. J., 25
Perret-Catipovic, M., 2–3
Perry, D. G., 23
Perry, J. C., 8–9, 15
"Peter": clinical example, violence
    in care, 60–63

Pettit, G. S., 23
phobias and parent battering, 47
"Pierre": clinical example,
        bullying, 33–35
Pirkis, J., 75
Portman Clinic, xi
post-traumatic stress disorder, 43
powerlessness, 39
    and omnipotence and parent
        battering, 43, 54
practitioners, impact of suicidal
        adolescent on, 82–84
primary love, 44
prisoner(s), 59
    treatment of, ix
Pritchard, C., 75
projections, 62
projective identification, 23
"provocative victims", 23
psychiatric disorders and
        children in care, 58
psychosis and suicide risk, 76,
        82
purple hearts, 2

Qin, P., 76

Randall, P., 21
Rank, O., x
rational thinking deficit and
        suicide risk, 75
regressive arousal states and
        parent battering, 48
rejection, sense of, violence as
        defence against, 3
Renaud, J., 75
repression, 40
reverie, maternal, 23
Rigby, K., 23
risk-containment plan, 81
Rosen, I., xi
Rosen, P. M., 15–16

Sacco, F. C., 25
Sachs, H., x
sado-masochistic collusion in
        parent battering, 52, 54
SAD PERSONS mnemonic, 75–76
Salmivalli, C., 25–26
San Quentin California State
        Prison, x
scapegoating, 36
Schaal, C., 46
Scherzer, A. L., xv–xvi, 5–20
Schmideberg, M., xi
Schwartz, D., 23
secrecy, 16–17
self-abuse, 8
self-cutting and emotional
        deprivation, 15
self-destructive behaviour, 5–20,
        84
    clinical implications, 17–19
    definition, 6–9
    eating disorders as, 6–20
    and emotional deprivation, 15–
        17
    vs. "normal" adolescent
        development, 9–11
    self-harm as, 6–20
self-esteem, 60
self-harm, 3, 65
    and bulimia, 8
    deliberate, 8
    and depersonalization, 8
    gender differences in, 7–9
    self-cutting, clinical example:
        15-year-old girl, 18–19
    as self-destructive behaviour, 6–
        20
    self-injury, 8
    self-laceration, 8
    self-mutilation, 8
    self-poisoning, 8
    self-wounding, 8

self-harm (*continued*):
    and sexual abuse, 9
    and suicide, 8
separation:
    fear of, 15
    –individuation, failure in phase
        of, 16–17
sexual abuse, 60
    and self-harm, 9
    and suicide risk, 76
sexual orientation, factor in
        suicide risk, 76–77
shame:
    as catalyst for violence, 3
    sense of, violence as defence
        against, 3
Shea, S. C., 79
shoplifting, 8
Smith, G. L., 75
Smith, P. K., 21–26
social competence, lack of, and
        parent battering, 50
social exclusion, 29
social integration, poor, and
        parent battering, 50
socialization, 9
speed, 77
"S.S.": clinical example, parent
        battering, 53–54
Steinmetz, S. K., 45
Stern, S., 16
Stoller, R. J., 22
sublimation, 40
substance abuse and parent
        battering, 47
suicidality:
    clinical example: "Jane", 78
    and jealousy in
        countertransference,
        clinical example:
        "Andrew", 84

suicide:
    attempted, 73–85
        risk factors, 74–76
    "contagion", 76
    family history of, and suicide
        risk, 76
    and self-harm, 8
superego, 10
supervision, increased, and
        suicide risk, 82
"supportive team" and suicide
        risk, 80–82
Sutton, J., 25–26
symbiotic communication, 42
systemic perspective on bullying,
        21

Talbot, R., 60
"Tamara": clinical example,
        bullying, 30–31
Tantam, D., 8
tantrum(s), 43
Terr, L., 45
testosterone, 40
thinking, magical, 44
Thomas, A., 41
transitional object and self-harm,
        14
trauma:
    and brain function, 42
    early, 13
    infantile, 39–55
    theory, 45
truanting, 63
Twemlow, S. W., 22, 25

United States, 22
Urban, E., 11, 12

van der Kolk, B. A., 8–9, 15
Verrara, 26

victim:
    aggressive, 23
    passive, 23
    provocative, 23
victimization
    peer, 23
    see also bullying
victims, characteristics of, 21
Vienna Psycho-Analytical Society,
        x
violence:
    in care, 57–72
        clinical examples:
            "Jeremy", 68–71
            "Gavin", 63–68
            "Peter", 60–63
    parental, 43
    in schools, 21–37
Vogel, D., 43
Voice for the Child in Care, 57

Walsh, B. W., 15–16

Ward, T., 75, 76, 79
Warren, F., 8–9
Waslick, B., 75, 76
Welldon, E., xi
Westwick, A., ix, xi
White, M., 79
Whittaker, J., 8
Williams, P., 25
Wilson, S., 58
Winnicott, D. W., 10, 12, 14
    on aggressive impulses, 44
    on infantile distress, 41
    on holding function of mother,
        73–74
    on transitional object, 14
withdrawal and disconnection in
        countertransference and
        suicidality, 83
wrist-cutting, 8
Wyler, I. L., 24

Young People in Care, 66